There has never been a mor
Christians and the body of C
sity of agreement. The Greek word *agree* means to sound
or say the same thing. We derive our word *symphony*
from the Greek word. The adversary has yet to see God's
end-time army united as one. It is for this reason that Dr.
Ron Phillips and his son Ronnie Phillips Jr. have put their
minds together to present to you this book, *The Power of
Agreement*. Don't just read this book; put it into practice
and watch the level of your spiritual authority grow.

—PERRY STONE JR.
FOUNDER AND PRESIDENT, VOICE OF EVANGELISM
HOST, *MANNA-FEST* TV PROGRAM

We don't just need God—we need to be in agreement with
Him. This may seem so obvious that it shouldn't even be
necessary to point out, but the facts tell us a different
story. Plans are unrealized, hopes and dreams are unful-
filled, and purposes are frustrated because believers fall
short of achieving agreement with God. But this is only
half of the problem.

The other part of the equation is that we need to be in
agreement with one another. And in our fast-paced, tech-
savvy, me-centered culture, agreement with those around
us can be difficult to accomplish.

In their book *The Power of Agreement*, the father-and-
son team of Ron Phillips and Ronnie Phillips Jr. addresses
these concerns with honesty and clarity. They present the
concepts of agreement with God and others concisely and
persuasively as a fundamental key to experiencing a life of
maximum effectiveness and influence.

—ROD PARSLEY
PASTOR, WORLD HARVEST CHURCH
HOST, *BREAKTHROUGH*
NEW YORK TIMES BEST-SELLING AUTHOR, *CULTURALLY
INCORRECT*

The Power *of Agreement* is a book that will bless you and
make your life richer. Being in agreement with God and

His Word, families and friends, your church and leaders, will help your life to be more satisfying and blessed. I salute Pastors Ron and Ron Jr. for their efforts to help the body of Christ.

—DODIE OSTEEN
COFOUNDER, LAKEWOOD CHURCH
HOUSTON, TEXAS

In 2012 Ronnie Phillips Jr. heard a word from the Lord that ended up saving the life of his father, Dr. Ron Phillips. Walking in the *power of agreement* is necessary to hearing the voice of the Lord and the promptings of the Holy Spirit, and it is evident that the Phillips family not only teaches on this principle but also lives by these principles as a family and a ministry. Agreement is the bridge to the supernatural!

—RABBI CURT LANDRY
CURT LANDRY MINISTRIES

As I read through Dr. Ron Phillips and Ronnie Phillips Jr.'s book, *The Power of Agreement*, I realized they speak about one of the most necessary eternal truths in the world—the power of agreement for yourself and your family!

This book fully teaches how to destroy the satanic weapon of disagreement that works against you! The Phillips's journey through trials vs. triumphs, challenges vs. victory, loss vs. gain, separation vs. unity, and disagreement vs. agreement will teach you how to cause Satan's number one weapon to "never prosper against you"! This is a book that I will use for myself.

—WALTER HALLAM
PRESIDENT AND SENIOR PASTOR
ABUNDANT LIFE CHRISTIAN CENTER OF LAMARQUE INC.
ABUNDANT LIFE CHRISTIAN CENTER—ALICE
CHAMPIONS LIFE CHRISTIAN CHURCH OF DALLAS INC.

THE

POWER OF

AGREEMENT

THE
POWER OF
AGREEMENT

RON PHILLIPS
and RONNIE PHILLIPS Jr.

CHARISMA
HOUSE

Most CHARISMA HOUSE BOOK GROUP products are available at special quantity discounts for bulk purchase for sales promotions, premiums, fund-raising, and educational needs. For details, write Charisma House Book Group, 600 Rinehart Road, Lake Mary, Florida 32746, or telephone (407) 333-0600.

THE POWER OF AGREEMENT by Ron Phillips and Ronnie Phillips Jr.
Published by Charisma House
Charisma Media/Charisma House Book Group
600 Rinehart Road
Lake Mary, Florida 32746
www.charismahouse.com

Cover design by Justin Evans
Design Director: Bill Johnson

Visit the author's website at www.abbashouse.com.

Library of Congress Cataloging-in-Publication Data:
An application to register this book for cataloging has been submitted to the Library of Congress.
International Standard Book Number: 978-1-62136-542-6
E-book ISBN: 978-1-62136-543-3

While the author has made every effort to provide accurate telephone numbers and Internet addresses at the time of publication, neither the publisher nor the author assumes any responsibility for errors or for changes that occur after publication.

First edition

14 15 16 17 18 — 987654321
Printed in the United States of America

In dedication to Clay and Susie Simmons, who lost a son but found grace in the midst of tragedy. Agreement is unity despite what happens to you. I believe they have discovered the power of agreement.

CONTENTS

PROLOGUE

In Remembrance of Dietrich Bonhoeffer

Dietrich Bonhoeffer died in his late thirties at the hand of Hitler's Nazi regime. It was just days before the liberation of Europe from Nazi tyranny. Bonhoeffer was truly a martyr for Christ and for the true church. Bonhoeffer had safe refuge in America yet in answer to his own convictions returned to his beloved Germany for the sake of the church. Bonhoeffer's classic, *The Cost of Discipleship*, does not mince words or play games with the matter of the church and the church's life. Who can forget his true definition of the call to discipleship? "When Christ calls a man, He bids him come and die."[1]

Beyond this courageous conviction there was something more that summoned this man to martyrdom. Second only to Christ was Bonhoeffer's deep love for and desire to preserve a remnant of the true church in Germany. The state church had exchanged the cross for the swastika and politically correct accommodation to the wicked regime of Hitler.

The hope for Germany during those dark days was the true fellowship of the confessing church. Eric Metaxas tracks that struggle in his award-winning biography called *Bonhoeffer*.[2]

Bonhoeffer led an underground seminary to train ministers for a post-war, post-Hitler, post-Nazi church! A brief chronicle of this experience is found in his book, *Life Together*.

In this book he sets forth a model of the true unity, agreement, and fellowship of the church as lived out in that seminary setting.[3]

Bonhoeffer's hope for the war-torn Germany was the true church. That is also my hope for America and our Western civilization. National Socialism is the government elite taking over everything and squashing human freedom and initiative. This includes the church. American patriots died that the church in the West might be free, unencumbered by the ruthless assaults of a secular, power-hungry political class.

The German church compromised and divided, following Hitler to ruin, with the exception of Bonhoeffer's students. What is best in the German church today is his legacy.

The American church is in trouble, losing her distinctive place and falling into a Christless, crossless culture!

I, as Bonhoeffer did, rest my hope in Christ and His church. For true renewal there must be a rediscovery and recovery of true togetherness with Jesus Christ and one another. This unity releases the potential of supernatural transformation. St. Paul's ideal of a return of God's power and glory rested upon his abiding faith that the church Jesus built will survive and thrive.

I therefore dedicate this book to Dietrich Bonhoeffer and all who love the ecclesia! May we all learn the joy of living life in agreement.

Now to Him who is able to do exceedingly abundantly
above all that we ask or think, according to the power
that works in us, to Him be glory in the church by
Christ Jesus to all generations, forever and ever. Amen.
—EPHESIANS 3:20–21

ACKNOWLEDGMENTS

W E WANT TO thank the splendid staff and membership of Abba's House for all of their support. Especially we want to thank Reverend Denise Craig, Reverend Angie McGregor, and Reverend Bill Marion for their support. Also, we want to thank Andrea Ridge for all typing efforts. Finally, we would like to honor the memory of Dr. John Osteen and the model he left in his wife and children for living out the supernatural power of agreement.

FOREWORD

AS A FELLOW pastor I have seen the unfortunate devastation that division has caused countless individuals and families. This is why I am so excited to endorse *The Power of Agreement* by Ron Phillips and Ronnie Phillips Jr. as a book that will help you experience God's best by living in agreement with God and with others. Get your highlighter ready as you learn these life-changing truths.

—JENTEZEN FRANKLIN
SENIOR PASTOR, FREE CHAPEL
AUTHOR, *NEW YORK TIMES* BEST SELLER *FASTING*

BEGINNING THE JOURNEY
TO AGREEMENT

Relationship is not a project, it is a grace.[1]
—THOMAS MOORE, FROM *SOUL MATES*

O NLY WHEN OUR relationship with God moves beyond casual to intimate may we truly discover who we are. Only when we understand what Plato meant when he said, "Know thyself," can we begin to connect with others in meaningful and fruitful ways.

In this book we will move from knowing God to knowing others, and then to making the right connections with people that bring supernatural blessing and good success into our lives. Here in this first section, Reverend Ronnie Phillips Jr. tears open his heart and unpacks his journey back to Jesus, back to his family, back to serving the true church, and back to his real identity. Prepare to be challenged and transformed. Everyone who has ever been hurt by a church, a trusted friend, or a leader will resonate with the truth God reveals in this book.

Section two unfolds the key to every relationship and intimacy. Intimacy begins with one's connection with God. Finally, in section three we will translate all of this truth to our home and to the various places we live our lives.

Both Ronnie and I had crisis experiences with the Holy Spirit that changed us and have deepened our lifelong relationship. The unrelenting pull of the Holy Spirit has given us both a deeper love for people, and together we are becoming true shepherds who value relationships with others over our own personal means and agenda. Together we have fashioned this entire book.

I am blessed that through all Ronnie's ups and downs we remained very close. Also, his respect and love for his mother never waned. She prayed for Ronnie, and a friend of hers saw Ronnie in a vision before we knew his gender!

Ronnie has a peculiar tremble that comes upon him when moved by the Spirit. He trembles in God's presence. As God has shaken him and me, we believe what follows can release the miracle promises of agreement found in Scripture.

In 1989, as a Southern Baptist pastor, my life was interrupted, shattered, and put back together by the baptism of the Holy Spirit. This experience changed me, challenged me, and caused me to help people get free of the enemy and powerfully connected to others in the church. This whole story is given in my book *Everyone's Guide to Demons and Spiritual Warfare.*

Twenty-three years later I went in for a stress test and discovered I was within three days of death with a complete arterial blockage. Shortly before my life-saving surgery, my pastor and son, Reverend Ronnie Phillips Jr., laid hands on me and prayed for me. Only a month before he had been named my successor by our board. Now, with our church going through the recession and many pressures, I seemed to be down for the count.

"Daddy," he said, "what do you want me to do?"

I said, "I have thirty-two years of equity. Stand in that favor and lead the church."

Not only did he lead, he set the church on a new course of anointing and growth.

Ronnie's presence at my side is a miracle of God's restoration and the unrelenting power of authentic relationships. See, a few years before he had lost touch with God and the church, but not with me. God called him back "not a moment too soon."

Journey with us into a supernatural season of restored relationships. Let's begin with Ronnie Jr.'s comeback.

—RON PHILLIPS

Chapter 1

A LIFE IN DISAGREEMENT

By Ronnie Phillips Jr.

IT WAS A warm spring afternoon in June of 2005. I was just finishing up with my weekly duties at a local insurance company where I had worked for seven years. Once a week my friends and I would meet at a local bar, have a few drinks (some weeks more than others), and then call it a night. We would use any football, basketball, or baseball game as an excuse to drink and celebrate. This miserable existence is what most people experience from week to week. They work in jobs they aren't passionate about and hope to find joy in some drinks, entertainment, and laughs. Many times the people we surround ourselves with aren't encouraging us to grow and become something more than we ever imagined. These friends choose to accept our camouflaged smiles and pretend bliss, and in exchange we accept their illusion as well. This was my life for many years.

I was married at a young age, and I felt somewhat successful climbing a corporate latter. Everything on the outside seemed great, like I had surpassed all the opinions of man, but something was missing deep inside. My marriage was in disarray. My job had plateaued. My relationships with my Father and God's people were in shambles. I had spent the last five years mad at God, mad at church people, and mad at myself. I had felt a passion to help people and to serve others since I was a little boy, but I felt extremely inadequate due to many failures and broken dreams.

As evening approached, I felt the Holy Spirit tugging at me as I drove past Abba's House, where our people were building the church my father had dreamed of and the foundation was being poured. The Holy Spirit spoke to my spirit and said, "There lies your destiny. You are needed there now."

This was very strange to me as I hadn't been praying, studying, or attending church consistently, which I thought was the only way God would speak to man. Forgive me; I was raised Baptist. I had long given up on the dream of pastoring, and I was far too bitter at the church to represent or serve the church. This inner voice or impression grew louder and more real as the night went on. I drank more than usual to try to drown out this impression from the Holy Spirit. Sitting at the bar that night, I fell under conviction, a deep sense of guilt. I felt that I had been a failure and that most of the people I had surrounded myself with weren't real friends. They truly didn't know the pain of what I was going through. I felt lonely, defeated, and frustrated.

I got home around midnight. My wife and I began to fight, which was pretty typical on the nights I would go out with the guys. I looked in the mirror and began to cry and tremble.

The Holy Spirit became more aggressive as the night went on. Things were about to "get real" at my house.

The Lord began to remind me of the call He had placed on my life at eight years old. This was before all the abuse, sin, anger, and frustration, and before people in authority began chipping away at my love for people. I felt the Lord was speaking to me in an urgent manner and that this was my last opportunity to repent and follow Him. I fell to my knees and began to unleash angry words toward God about things I had done, things that had been done to me, and things for which I had blamed God. At one point I was yelling at God about my own father (Ron Phillips).

Dad has always been my hero and my best friend, but I had grown very bitter at him as well. I felt as if both of my parents were ashamed of me and that they had helped so many other people in ministry but refused to embrace me.

After two hours of this, my wife was extremely scared; she had never seen me behave like this before. Luckily, my son Trey, who was four years old at the time and my only reason for living prior to this night, did not wake up during any of this. Kelly threatened to call my dad during this ordeal. I yelled back, "Call him—he won't come!" Sure enough, she called, he answered, and he came.

This was pretty amazing, as Dad sleeps like a rock and rarely answers the phone during the day, much less late at night. Looking back I am sure this was very painful for my father because he had often been exposed to drunken rants by his own father as a child. I'm sure when he pulled up it felt like a stroll down memory lane for him.

When he came in, I immediately attacked him with my words about the ministry and how he was gone too much and

7

how he didn't stand up for me during key times in my life. I didn't stay there long. I began to apologize over and over, "I am not worthy to be your son." I confessed and repented about certain things I had done to shame our family. This became a life-changing night. We prayed, cried, and forgave each other. My wife and I repented to each other. My dad and I rekindled our strong bond. Most importantly, I repented to God and gave my life to Him once and for all.

Life in disagreement is not a very fun place to be. Happiness is temporary, and you live in fear of losing what little you have. You live under a heaviness that clouds your judgment and rules your emotions.

The next four months were very difficult. Each day I wanted to quit. I was embarrassed when I would attend church because I was afraid of what others might think. (My father had asked me to preach in four months from this experience. I believe he did this to give me some sort of goal or something to look forward to.) It was during this time that I learned the true meaning of grace. I learned that grace is undeserved, unmerited favor. I learned that Jesus came to this earth for me and people like me. He came for the unwanted, abandoned, abused—the sinner. I found purpose in Jesus Christ. I discovered the power of agreement. God had called me to the brokenhearted. He began to change my mind-set.

I preached my first message from John 5 called "Porch." It was a simple message about how the church ought to be a place where the sick, lame, blind, hurt, abused, and addicted are welcome as they wait for their miracle. The church was packed, including the balcony, which didn't happen often on a Sunday night. This showed me that while I experienced a lot of pain and hurt from church people as a child, there was a significant number of people who were *for* this underdog with Jr. attached to his name.

Before I preached we sang "How Great Thou Art," which was my grandfather's favorite song. I was reminded of what a compassionate, calm man he was despite the deep hurts he experienced from his upbringing. He had become a servant of Christ after suffering from a serious drinking problem when my dad was a child. But I am convinced that he continued to live with the pain from his past that had caused my father many problems.

That night I stood there in that sanctuary, pressed between the legacy of my father and the personality of my grandfather. I was overwhelmed by the significance of this night. God was using me to heal the brokenhearted, bring freedom to the captives, and reach people the church had given up on. How did God choose to do this with me? Many of the friends from my past attended this service and their lives were radically changed because of what God did and what they saw in this scared young preacher.

I must say that when I got my relationship with God in line with His Word, my other relationships followed suit. My wife and I have been married for twelve years, and we have three wonderful boys. My dad and I now serve as pastors of Abba's House together, as a threefold cord that cannot be broken. I'm a better son to my heavenly Father, a better husband to my wife, a better father to my children, and a better friend because of the transformational change that occurred seven years ago on my bathroom floor. It started with the voice of God, which led to conviction, which led to repentance, which led to restoration in my relationships, and which eventually led me to redemption and reflection.

What has sustained me over the course of the last seven years is my relationship with God; my wife and three boys; my relationship with my father; and some old and new friends. I am surrounded by people who want to see me reach my fullest potential in life. I thank God for a life that is now in unity, agreement, and harmony with the world around me. When I hear the words of the song by country music artist Tim McGraw, "Not a Moment Too Soon," I think of our Lord and Savior Jesus Christ and how He rescued me.

The Lord came to seek and save the lost. When you come into agreement with Him, your life will count. You may not feel worthy, but the Lord desperately wants to have a relationship with His creation. He created you for more. Embrace it and begin to walk in it.

Chapter 2

THE EMPTINESS WE SHARE

By Ronnie Phillips Jr.

T HE HUMAN CONDITION today is a result of the greatest breach ever in relationships—the fall of man in Eden. All the tragedy, emptiness, loneliness, and unworthiness in the human experience is rooted in man's fatal choice to break fellowship with God. These are the awful emotions and feelings all in the human family share.

One of the most valuable resources in life is the strength found in quality relationships. Everyone is born with an emptiness inside that can only be filled by the transforming power of God through His Son, Jesus Christ. Many of us try to fill this emptiness with meaningless relationships, minute accomplishments, and things that bring us temporary pleasure. We all thirst for a long-lasting relationship with Jesus Christ that meets all of our spiritual and emotional needs, but sometimes we don't recognize the Source of that thirst. Sometimes the Lord sends us people in our lives with "skin on" to help us get to the "well" of living water, but sometimes the enemy sends us what the apostle Paul calls "stumbling blocks" (Rom. 14) that keep us from our God-given destiny. So how do we deal with this emptiness? It starts with a relationship with Christ, but it doesn't end there. In this chapter I want to deal with emptiness, loneliness, and unworthiness. The reason many of us aren't experiencing real joy is because we feel empty, lonely, or feel unworthy to walk in the favor God has for us as His children. The world bursts with a population of seven billion people, yet so many in this throng of humanity suffer emptiness, loneliness, and unworthiness. Jesus offers a solution in John 7:37 (NIV):

> On the last and greatest day of the Feast, Jesus stood and said in a loud voice, "If anyone is thirsty, let him come to me and drink."

My question to you is, Are you thirsty? "Thirsty for what?" you might ask. Thirsty for a life lived in agreement with God the Father, Son, and Holy Spirit.

THE LONELINESS WE SHARE

My grandfather Billy Baker was an avid listener of Hank Williams Sr., a lovesick soul who died a tragic death in the back of a Cadillac at age twenty-nine. I guess my grandfather's love for this lovesick soul was passed down to me. Hank Williams Sr. was a man diagnosed with a degenerative disc disease[1] and an even more difficult disease that was undiagnosed called loneliness. He wrote and sang many sad songs such as "Lovesick Blues" and "Lost Highway." But Hank Sr.'s most famous song, "I'm So Lonesome I Could Cry," says it all.

If you know the man behind the song then you most definitely will become emotional when you listen to his music. Hank Williams Sr. had a very rough life, and his relationship with his estranged wife, Audrey, was very tumultuous to say the least.[2] There were all sorts of stories about their marital indiscretions that are now part of country music legend. How could the same man with an anointing to write and sing gospel music like his 1948 release, "I Saw the Light," end up dying alone in the back of a Cadillac? I don't believe he was ever able to get over this disease called loneliness.

Have you ever felt alone like Hank Williams Sr.? Have you ever felt alone in this life? Is it possible that our Creator ever felt that way? We know that Jesus felt alone at times, but what about our Abba Father?

Systematic theology teaches us that God is self-sufficient and doesn't have any needs, which in essence is true. God doesn't need you or me. But I believe God gets lonely too, and He does want us. God wants to be our friend. He longs for us to feel the same way about Him that He feels about us. God wants to be looked at as our reward, not our ritual. That is what church has become for many believers, a ritual. It is supposed to be a well of "living water" where we meet with other friends and experience His presence so that we can fulfill the purpose He has for us. Instead it has become a place of walls, legalism, and religion.

God doesn't want us to be lonely. He desires to have a relationship with His creation. God found pleasure in creating our world and placing us in it. I believe that friendship is a hidden attribute of the deity. We are God's gift to Himself, and friendship is the greatest treasure we can give or receive from one another.

UNWORTHINESS WE SHARE

Adam and Eve were God's first friends, but after they sinned they hid themselves from Him because they felt unworthy. Many of you are hiding from God because you are empty, lonely, and feel unworthy. Jesus Christ wants to deliver you from those feelings and take long walks with you again.

> And they heard the sound of the LORD God walking in the garden in the cool of the day, and Adam and his wife hid themselves from the presence of the LORD God among the trees of the garden. Then the LORD God called to Adam and said to him, "Where are you?" So he said, "I heard Your voice in the garden, and I was afraid because I was naked; and I hid myself."
> —GENESIS 3:8–10

Have you ever felt like Adam or Eve? I know I have. The reason I ran from God for nearly six years was because I let the enemy convince me that I wasn't worthy. The enemy wants nothing more than to destroy God's children. His method for destruction often begins with an accusation. My father and I desperately want you to come back into agreement with God and experience life together with the God who created you. His love for you is so great that He sent His Son, Jesus Christ, to die an agonizing death for your sins. Through the power of the Holy Spirit, He can transform your life from loneliness to togetherness, from empty to full, and from unworthy to worthy.

This is the first step toward living life in that supernatural place of unity and agreement. None of us is worthy in and of ourselves. We have been made worthy through the sacrifice of Jesus Christ. Some Christians today act as if they have arrived, as if they have achieved the pinnacle of Christianity; but they haven't. In this life we will always be pressing toward the mark and moving forward. This continues until the day we are called home to glory. We don't ever fully arrive on this side of eternity. It is important that you understand and embrace this transforming knowledge of God before you move toward intimacy with Him, your friends, and your family.

THE TRINITY

The transforming theology of relationships can be found in the Trinity, the nature and unity of God the Father, the Son, and the Holy Spirit. He is one in three and three in one. It is impossible for God to be any less than the Trinity. There are many pictures of this transforming theology in the Bible. At the baptism of Jesus the Spirit descended on Him, and the voice of God the Father burst through the heavens identifying Jesus Christ as His Son (Matt. 3:16). Jesus said in John 14:16 that the Father would send another Comforter, the Holy Spirit. In Matthew 28 the disciples were told to baptize in the name of the Father, Son, and the Holy Spirit. Jesus was referred to as the Son of Man and Immanuel (God with us).

Within the doctrine of the Trinity (*trinitas* in Latin) I see a picture of relationships. I see unity, favor, and blessing in action. When the triune God begins to move, favor is released and wonderful things begin to happen in our relationships. The first thing you must know about God is that He is our Father. Consider Isaiah 9:6 (NIV):

> For to us a child is born, to us a son is given, and the government will be on his shoulders. And he will be

called Wonderful Counselor, Mighty God, **Everlasting Father**, Prince of Peace.

Father

The Father represents our covering. God is a shield and He provides a safe haven for His sons and daughters. The reason so many people face difficulty in life is because they don't have a father in their life. This applies to people who either had an absentee father or a father who abandoned them, and now they struggle with extreme insecurity and inferiority. If those things aren't dealt with spiritually, then the son or daughter will take on an "orphan spirit" and never truly have the creativity and confidence to achieve greatness. In essence, the Father represents our covering, our ability to create, and our confidence to complete the tasks at hand.

> Because you are sons, God sent the Spirit of his Son into our hearts, the Spirit who calls out, *"Abba, Father."*
> —GALATIANS 4:6, NIV, EMPHASIS ADDED

Son

The Son (Jesus Christ) represents the drive to get up and get going. The Son provides the motivation to attempt and achieve greatness, but it must happen in conjunction with the Father. You must first have a covering before you can embark on your destiny. That covering will give you the confidence to create. The spirit of the Son will give you the drive to build on the legacy of your Father. This will give you the motivation that you need to finish the work. We know that Jesus Christ finishes whatever He begins.

Jesus said to them, "My food is to do the will of Him who sent Me, and to finish His work."

—JOHN 4:34

For the works which the Father has given Me to finish— the very works that I do—bear witness of Me, that the Father has sent Me.

—JOHN 5:36

When you embrace the Son, you embrace the motivation to finish.

God has raised this Jesus to life, and we are all witnesses of the fact. Exalted to the right hand of God, he has received from the Father the promised Holy Spirit and has poured out what you now see and hear.

—ACTS 2:32–33, NIV

Holy Spirit

The Holy Spirit is the Third Person of His deity and represents divine intellect. There are people who are operating under the anointing of the Father, Son, and Holy Spirit who are less qualified, less educated, and less gifted, but they are being blessed more than others because they have learned the blessing that comes from being in covenant with God the Father, Son, and Holy Spirit. The Holy Spirit gives you the movement you need to advance His kingdom and the ministry God has for you. The Holy Spirit represents momentum. It can't be explained how God lines things up for His people who are operating in covenant with "all" of who He is. The Holy Spirit represents divine favor, grace, and greatness. The Holy Spirit makes our work easier. The Holy Spirit is the glue that brings the Father and the Son together to come "upon" us.

And I will ask the Father, and he will give you another Counselor to be with you forever—the Spirit of truth. The world cannot accept him, because it neither sees him nor knows him. But you know him, for he lives with you and will be in you.

—JOHN 14:16–17, NIV

SO, ARE YOU THIRSTY?

I hope so. When you get thirsty enough, then God will open up the floodgates and send you rivers of living water. So many people operate in one of the three characteristics of His deity, but if you want to achieve greatness and form relationships that will last and mean something in heaven, then you must operate under the authority of Abba Father, the transforming power of His Son that will cause you to finish, mixed with divine favor, power, and supernatural momentum that comes from the Holy Spirit.

The first step is to accept Christ as your Lord and Savior, or come back to Him by asking Him to forgive you and transform your life from the inside out. Just pray this simple prayer: *Dear Lord Jesus, please forgive me of my sins. Come into my heart and save me. You are my Creator, my Father, my Savior, and my Friend. I surrender my life to You and ask You to fill me with Your precious Holy Spirit. Lead me in the paths of righteousness and use me for Your glory. Amen.*

Chapter 3

THE MIRACLE OF AGREEMENT

By Ron Phillips

T HE MIRACLE KEY to everything we need in business, in
our nation, in our homes, in our churches, and in our
individual lives will be revealed in the pages before
you. Satan has deceived believers and nonbelievers into a
self-centered narcissism that has brought destruction and
waste. When you follow the enemy's tracks, his goal is always
"divide and conquer."

In Eden Satan brought death, dealing division to Adam
and Eve and plunging the human race into the Fall.

At Babel Satan sought to use the miracle principle of
unity to lead another rebellion against God. The ancient
ruler Nimrod sought to usurp God's throne, as had Satan,
by building a tower. Consequently division came and the
nations began to war against one another.

Abraham divided his family by siring a boy named Ishmael,
the father of the Arab nation. This division now spans more

than three thousand years with the Middle East still raging with war in Syria and Afghanistan, civil war in Iraq, and unrest in Israel. This reflection of a divided humanity will culminate with the end-time war of Armageddon. American troops have warred in the Middle East for over a decade. The terror attacks on our nation are a result of this ancient division.

The division of Jacob's sons and the selling of Joseph into slavery led to famine and shortage for Israel. This would only be remedied by the restoration of these brothers.

The captivities of both Israel and Judah took place after their division into two separate kingdoms under Jeroboam and Rehoboam. Israel could mark its decline from that breach in family relationship.

When Jesus arrived on the scene, the faith of Abraham was divided into Pharisees and Sadducees. They had wrecked the faith, and now the nation lived in slavery under Herod and Rome!

THE CROSS AND UNITY

Jesus came to die for individuals, but His Cross also made possible miracle-working relationships. His Cross reconciles all divisions.

Before His death and resurrection, Jesus gave a hint about miracle power in Matthew 18:19–20: "Again I say to you that if two of you agree on earth concerning anything that they ask, it will be done for them by My Father in heaven. For where two or three are gathered together in My name, I am there in the midst of them."

Read this promise and see its potential. If we can agree, anything becomes possible!

Satan has convinced the Western world that individualism, self-assertion, and self-interest are the way. In the communist world he has divided the people into the educated elites and the so-called workers or masses. Here humans lose their souls.

The truth is that the Cross redeems the individual and then reconciles that person with all the redeemed. In this new level of "agreement" miracles become possible.

In John 15:1–8 Jesus teaches us that connections count:

> "I am the true vine, and My Father is the vinedresser. Every branch in Me that does not bear fruit He takes away; and every branch that bears fruit He prunes, that it may bear more fruit. You are already clean because of the word which I have spoken to you. Abide in Me, and I in you. As the branch cannot bear fruit of itself, unless it abides in the vine, neither can you, unless you abide in Me.
>
> "I am the vine, you are the branches. He who abides in Me, and I in him, bears much fruit; for without Me you can do nothing. If anyone does not abide in Me, he is cast out as a branch and is withered; and they gather them and throw them into the fire, and they are burned. If you abide in Me, and My words abide in you, you will ask what you desire, and it shall be done for you. By this My Father is glorified, that you bear much fruit; so you will be My disciples."

First, we must "abide in the vine." Using the image of a vineyard, Jesus views believers as clusters of tasty grapes on a flourishing vine; each grape is delicious, but together they can produce something more valuable: wine. This teaching reflects the Old Testament prophecies of God's family.

In Isaiah 5, the vineyard fails because of the divisive power of sin and produces a rotten vintage. God removes the protective hedge, and the vineyard is wasted!

Later, Isaiah reminds the people of the favor that is released in the cluster of grapes:

> Thus says the LORD: "As the new wine is found in the cluster, and one says, 'Do not destroy it, for a blessing is in it,' so will I do for My servants' sake, that I may not destroy them all."
>
> —ISAIAH 65:8

The prophet Micah mourns the loss of unity under the same image of the cluster of grapes:

> Woe is me! For I am like those who gather summer fruits, like those who glean vintage grapes; there is no cluster to eat of the first-ripe fruit which my soul desires. The faithful man has perished from the earth, and there is no one upright among men. They all lie in wait for blood; every man hunts his brother with a net.
>
> —MICAH 7:1–2

God is looking for the cluster and instead finds brother pitted against brother. This terrible scene shows how the blessing is forfeited and mourns the absence of new wine!

No wonder Jesus did such extensive teaching in John 15 on the vine and branches. It is amazing that Jesus uses the word *agreement* to describe our relationships.

The Greek word is *sumphoneo. Sum* is the word *together,* and *phoneo* is *voice* or *say.* We get our word *symphony* from this word. It means to let the same word of faith go forth from all of us in harmony. Every instrument in an orchestra is different, but when they are led by a capable conductor, the music is miraculous. This is the kind of harmony that is sweet to the ears of God. This kind of relationship makes miracles possible! God loves this kind of unity!

> Behold, how good and how pleasant it is
> For brethren to dwell together in unity!
> It is like the precious oil upon the head,
> Running down on the beard,
> The beard of Aaron,
> Running down on the edge of his garments.
> It is like the dew of Hermon,
> Descending upon the mountains of Zion;
> For there the Lord commanded the blessing—
> Life forevermore.
>
> —Psalm 133

In this psalm we learn that God commands not "a" blessing but "the" blessing when He beholds a people in unity. This psalm gives a prophetic view of the church clothed in the garments of the High Priest, with the anointing of power flowing from the Head, Jesus. As the church walks in unity, blessings flow off the Head to the hem of the garment. What a picture and promise.

Jesus came to bring reconciliation. In the Sermon on the Mount, Jesus declares that our offerings will not bring a harvest until we "reconcile with our brothers." (Matthew 5:24: "Leave your gift there before the altar, and go your way. First be reconciled to your brother, and then come and offer your gift.")

Jesus's prayer in John 17 is a cry for unity. This was what was on His great heart right before His bloody death. This whole prayer is in the plural, including us all! Note the following cry from the heart of Jesus:

> "I do not pray for these alone, but also for those who will believe in Me through their word; that they all may be one, as You, Father, are in Me, and I in You; that they also may be one in Us, that the world may believe that You sent Me. And the glory which You gave Me I have given them, that they may be one just as We are one: I in them, and You in Me; that they may be made perfect in one, and that the world may know that You have sent Me, and have loved them as You have loved Me.
>
> "Father, I desire that they also whom You gave Me may be with Me where I am, that they may behold My glory which You have given Me; for You loved Me before the foundation of the world."
>
> —JOHN 17:20–24

Notice that unity precedes the glory!

THE POWERFUL PROMISES OF LIVING IN AGREEMENT

The words *reconcile* and *reconciliation* are echoed by St. Paul in his letters to the church. First, Paul sees the Cross as the great unifier.

> For if when we were enemies we were reconciled to God through the death of His Son, much more, having been reconciled, we shall be saved by His life. And not only that, but we also rejoice in God through our Lord Jesus Christ, through whom we have now received the reconciliation.
>
> —ROMANS 5:10–11

Here Paul reveals that we are now reconciled to God and to one another. Being in unity with God and one another releases infinite possibilities for us as believers.

1. Unity brings down all walls and releases peace.

> For He Himself is our peace, who has made both one, and has broken down the middle wall of separation.
>
> —EPHESIANS 2:14

2. Unity forges a new humanity with tremendous possibilities.

> Having abolished in His flesh the enmity, that is, the law of commandments contained in ordinances, so as to create in Himself one new man from the two, thus making peace.
>
> —EPHESIANS 2:15

3. Unity was won by Christ on the cross as He endured all our hostilities against one another.

When we live in hostility toward our fellow believers, we crucify Christ again! In Galatians 2:1–19, Paul speaks of the destructive division Peter wrought when leaders from the church in Jerusalem came to Antioch and Peter would not sit with the non-Jews. It was this instance of terrible disunity that caused Paul to rebuke Peter. Paul's answer to this disunity is that we must be dead to it.

> I have been crucified with Christ; it is no longer I who live, but Christ lives in me; and the life which I now live in the flesh I live by faith in the Son of God, who loved me and gave Himself for me.
>
> —GALATIANS 2:20

We must be crucified to divisive behavior toward others.

4. Unity gives us access into God's presence.

> For through Him we both have access by one Spirit to the Father. Now, therefore, you are no longer strangers and foreigners, but fellow citizens with the saints and members of the household of God, having been built on the foundation of the apostles and prophets, Jesus Christ Himself being the chief cornerstone, in whom the whole building, being fitted together, grows into a holy temple in the Lord.
>
> —Ephesians 2:18–21

When we accepted Christ, we became the new temple of God!

5. Unity brings the highest level of spiritual fullness and power.

> In whom you also are being built together for a dwelling place of God in the Spirit.
>
> —Ephesians 2:22

When we are "built together," God lives in us! What awesome possibilities flow from such anointing.

THE SECRET OF SUPERNATURAL AGREEMENT

Several years ago I received a teaching from evangelist Damon Thompson called "Joined and Jointed" on the power of true unity. It quickened a deeper study of Paul's view of the church and her lack of power and miracle supply. As I studied, I found one word that exploded in my spirit about how unity can release the Father's supernatural supply. That word is *epichoregos*, and it is found hidden away in Ephesians 4:16:

> From whom the whole body, joined and knit together by what every joint supplies, according to the effective working by which every part does its share, causes growth of the body for the edifying of itself in love.

The New King James Version rightly translates the word as "supplies." It comes from two words *epi*, which means "upon," and *choregeo*, which means "one who fully furnishes a choir or dance team." Our English word *choreographer* comes from that word. A choreographer sets the stage and coordinates music, dance, and drama for the theater.

In the Greek world, theater was very important. In fact, our word *theater* came from the Greek language. In the Greco-Roman world, a *choregos* was also a "benefactor" who not only took care of all the stage arranging but also supplied all the finances, food, costuming, and salaries for the production.

Everyone who heard this word *epichoregos* understood that they needed God to be their *choregos*. The same word is found in Philippians 1:19, where Paul understood that resources from the Holy Spirit would be released for him by the prayers of his brothers and sisters.

The word is found also in the Second Letter to the Corinthians:

> Now may He who supplies seed to the sower, and bread for food, supply and multiply the seed you have sown and increase the fruits of your righteousness, while you are enriched in everything for all liberality, which causes thanksgiving through us to God.
> —2 CORINTHIANS 9:10–11

God is viewed here as the great *choregos*, who supplies "seed to the sower," "increase," and enrichment.

> If anyone speaks, let him speak as the oracles of God. If anyone ministers, let him do it as with the ability which God supplies, that in all things God may be glorified through Jesus Christ, to whom belong the glory and the dominion forever and ever. Amen.
>
> —1 PETER 4:11

Peter also declares that the gifts of the Holy Spirit come from our *choregos*. God "supplies" our gifts!

When the prodigal son came home we read in Luke 15:25 that there was music and dancing. The word *dancing* is *choroor*. The father of the prodigal put on a lavish production to welcome home his wayward son. Understand the Bible views God as our *choregos*, the One who directs and supplies our lives.

Understanding that, how does God release that provision to His people as His church? If we go back to Ephesians 4:16, we will see that the church is called a "body." Furthermore, the church is "fitly joined together" or *sunharmologoumenon* in the Greek. This is a compound word with *sum*, which means "together" or "*harmos*," from which our word *harmony* comes! The third part in this long word, *legos*, means "to speak." So here is a group that together, in harmony, says the same word of faith!

Now, watch this and learn how to receive your miracle. He goes on to say "every joint" (which is *hafees* in Greek, which means "ligament") "supplies." There is the miracle word. It is *epichoregeo*. When we are "together" in harmony, saying the same word of faith, God opens the window of heaven and pours out His abundant supply. Everything we need is available to us when we are rightly connected with one another. Every failure indicates a lack of right relationships.

This is why relationships are primary to God and to our lives. There is supernatural power in living life in agreement and unity with other believers.

Furthermore, for the church to be a twenty-first century temple that welcomes the Holy Spirit, we must live in this kind of unity.

Ephesians 2:21 says, "In whom the whole building, being fitted together, grows into a holy temple in the Lord."

This is the only other place sunharmologoumenon is used! God releases Holy Spirit power upon the group that speaks His promises in harmony.

AGREEMENT WITH GOD

*Every relationship that touches the soul
leads us into a dialogue with eternity...we
are being set face-to-face with divinity.*[1]
—THOMAS MOORE

H E STOOD CALMLY, alone and quiet in the middle of
the park. The gloom of the cloudy day cast a gray
shadow across his young face as he gazed steadily
into the sky. His hand firmly gripped a thin line of worn
string. The little boy had not gone unnoticed; many passersby
wished they could pause from their hurried day and join the
young boy. But the only one who stopped was the neighborhood bully.

Tauntingly he called out, "Hey, whatcha doin' out there,
Billy?"

Billy smiled and replied, "Flying my kite!"

Scanning the cloudy sky, the bully scoffed, "I don't see a thing! Bet your kite is long gone! Bet it's not even up there!"

Billy looked back at his string with another smile. "Oh, it's there, all right. You see, I can feel the tug."

That tug from above draws us to something beyond ourselves! The human soul and spirit have an instinctive desire to be connected beyond our natural world. It is possible to have your feet on the clay of the earth while your soul connects beyond the clouds to a life with God. Do you feel the tug?

You see, living life from a place of agreement and unity with the body of Christ always begins with our quest to know the Almighty! This truth stretches even beyond Scripture and other realms of study.

THE SCIENTIFIC QUEST

Science has calculated, measured, photographed, and listened to the sounds of the ages through mathematical equations, satellite and telescopic images, and radio waves in the quest to prove that there is a scientific explanation for our existence. While science can quantify much of the evidence for why the heavens and earth exist as they do, even those scientific explanations for every discovery point to a higher level of understanding that there was and is an intentional administration of the universe.

Albert Einstein (who may be considered the most renowned scientist of all time), despite his own immense mental power, bowed to the unfathomable nature of God. In 1932 he wrote the following:

The most beautiful and deepest experience a man can have is the sense of the mysterious. It is the underlying principle of religion as well as of all serious endeavors in art and science. He who never had this experience seems to me, if not dead, then at least blind. To sense that behind anything that can be experienced there is a something that our minds cannot grasp, whose beauty and sublimity reaches us only indirectly: this is religiousness. In this sense I am religious. To me it suffices to wonder at these secrets and to attempt humbly to grasp with my mind a mere image of the lofty structure of all there is.[2]

RELIGION'S QUEST

Islam, Judaism, and Christianity share the common goal of knowing God. Islam sees Allah as the monotheistic (the one and only) god who judges each follower for sins committed after the age of accountability, which is considered to take place when one reaches puberty. Reaching paradise is solely dependent on each follower's ability to do enough good deeds. There is no mediator between Allah and man in Islam; each person determines by his actions if he will go to paradise or hell. There are different sects in Islam, some peaceful, some moderate, and some violent.

Judaism is also classified as a monotheistic faith. Jews believe there is only one God—YHWH (Jehovah)—and He is present in our daily lives. Judaism teaches that each person, Jew and non-Jew, is created in the image of God with an infinite potential to do good. Jews do not believe that Jesus was the Messiah. In contrast to Islam, the focus of Judaism is on *olam ha-ze*, which means, "this world."[3] The Torah does not focus on the eternal life. Judaism, like Christianity, has several different approaches or sects. Reformed Jews are marked by the belief that the Jewish laws are guidelines, and that those guidelines should be regularly reviewed and modified and renewed based on the current culture of the day. Orthodox Jews would have been the Pharisees of the Bible. This sect strictly holds to the ethics and laws found in the Torah. The Kabbalistic Jews, who have come along in more recent history, believe in a mystic connection with God that is not unsimilar to what Christians believe, but without faith in Christ.[4] This sect is often misunderstood.

Messianic Judaism rose in the 1960s and 1970s. Generally Jews in this sect believe Jesus is the Son of God and the long-awaited Messiah of the Jews. Salvation is only received by accepting Jesus as Savior. Jewish laws and customs are cultural and necessary for faith in Jesus.[5]

Christianity has as its foundational doctrines the truth that there is only one triune God who is omniscient (knows everything), omnipotent (has all power), omnipresent (everywhere), and sovereign (has absolute lordship). Unlike Judaism and Islam, Christianity teaches that the Father, Holy Spirit, and Jesus Christ are the three parts of God. Jesus is the only way to the Father, our Mediator. And the Holy Spirit is God residing in His followers, enduing them with supernatural power.

Science recognizes there is a higher force that slung the galaxies into motion. Islam focuses on a grandiose afterlife reserved for those who are without sin. Judaism enjoys the blessing of doing good to others, and the reward of a life well lived. Christianity makes it possible for us to have life together with God now and in the eternal life to come through Jesus.

Chapter 4

THE QUEST FOR AGREEMENT WITH GOD

By Ron Phillips

C ENTURIES AGO THERE lived a young German monk. This devoted man took his holy orders seriously. His life was one of discipline. He had surrendered everything and viewed soberly the holy obligation of the church. Still, his struggling heart was empty. Finally, the young cleric decided that pilgrimage and penance was the way to God. He crawled up the high stairs in Rome where many made their pilgrimages, the staircase known as Scala Santa. Worn out and bloody from the journey, he still had no answer from God.[1]

Returning home, the young monk was browsing in a library when he came across a complete copy of the Latin Scriptures. He was astounded, for he had never held the entire Word of God in his hands, despite years of Bible study as a monk! That day the light came powerfully to Martin Luther as one verse from God's Word broke over his soul—"The just shall live by faith" (Rom. 1:17). Luther knew that Paul had written those words, echoing the prophet Habakkuk, to the church at Rome.[2]

Now, fifteen hundred years later, the same truth that had become almost smothered by church traditions exploded in his heart. In that moment of revelation, Martin Luther had a profound conversion and filling of the Holy Spirit. He moved from religious ritual to a personal relationship with Jesus. Now, at last, his quest for life together with God was made possible by the journey to Jesus. Luther went on to lead thousands of others to that same freedom!

An Empty Heart

Not unlike Luther, in 1989 I came to realize my own life had become one of religious works done to please God and to rise in denominational prestige and position. My early quest for life together with God had been swallowed by religious obligation. With a legalistic work ethic, I worked hard and achieved a measure of success, if nickels and noses were any measure in church life. After twenty-two years in the ministry I found myself empty and powerless.

My walls were lined with books I had mastered, a few I had written, degrees I had earned, and awards I'd received. Yet I had no close relationship with God. I had received His salvation, had dedicated my life to ministry, yet my soul was emaciated, starved for spiritual things. My pride in my knowledge kept me from talking about my hunger. I was opinionated and mean-spirited to those who didn't agree with me. Being right was more important to me than being righteous. God graciously began to allow disappointment and difficulty to exhaust my flesh. I became so miserable that I could no longer stand myself, nor did I feel I could continue as a pastor. My life had reached critical mass. Something had to give. Then, my life was overturned completely by what some call the baptism of the Holy Spirit. Up until that heavenly invasion, I had my faith neatly stacked into an orderly package. I believed that God did great things in the past and one day in heaven I would see Him. I was thoroughly orthodox and adamantly opposed the "mystics" who believed God could speak, act, and touch people like He did in the Book of Acts. Like a Pharisee, I had turned the written Word into an idol. I was a "Scripture expert" but a miserable failure at life.

At the moment I was ready to tender my resignation from the ministry, God met me in a hotel room in New Mexico! Oh, blessed invasion! Oh, divine disruption! I had a literal and personal awakening in the long night of my despair! God spoke to me, baptized me, filled me, and called me to an authentic relationship with Him.

From that new relationship would flow a new ministry, wild and free like a rushing river. This experience was not an end but the beginning of a fantastic quest for intimacy with Jesus. All my life I have been in hot pursuit of an intimate life dwelling together with God through the power of the Holy Spirit.

A DIFFICULT PATH

Visitors to the land of Israel have a profound experience if they walk through the old city in Jerusalem and experience the last steps of Jesus. Those are precious moments when eternity breaks through time and meets you in a real and tangible way! I remember one particular trip when my heart was already emotionally charged, having walked the Via

Dolorosa, the way of the cross. That day I had also toured "the pavement" under the Church of St. Anne, where scholars believe our Lord Jesus walked, endured trial, and shed drops of blood from His beating. The next stop was to be the Upper Room, where Jesus and His disciples shared the Passover meal. As we journeyed that day, a video crew from Israeli television followed our group. The reporter was a young Israeli woman. She asked me for an interview and got right to the point, asking, "Why are you here in Israel?" All of a sudden I felt a rush of wind in my face and the presence of Jesus flooded over me! This is what came out of my mouth: "I am in love with a Jew and wanted to see His country." Her shocked look changed to a warm smile when I added, "By the way, His name is Jesus of Nazareth. He lived here and rose again in this wonderful land. I am head over heels, passionately in love with Him." To my amazement that evening, there I was, all over Israel on the evening news declaring my love and passion for Jesus!

Late that night, I sat alone on the balcony of my hotel room overlooking the land where Jesus was born, educated, worshipped, preached to and healed the multitudes, served, suffered, died, and conquered death. The quest for life together cost Jesus everything. This was a difficult path. I fell to my knees on that hotel balcony and wept thinking about the fact that here, in this place, that timeless trail of blood was shed for my sins. The theological became personal, and I sobbed out my love for Jesus.

Why should those profound moments of passion be the exception rather than the norm? Sadly, over time, Jesus too often becomes only a subject to study, a religious code word, or simply an icon. But He really lived, and still lives! The glorious Christ who came down to earth two thousand years ago summoned me up to the stars that evening in Israel. It was a moment when the eternal dimension intersected with time and interrupted my schedule in order to manifest the lasting love that is found in life together with God.

FINDING A FOREVER FRIEND

God fills and empowers us to go on with our lives enjoying an intimate, daily walk with Him. Do we really believe that God allowed His beloved Son to be savagely beaten, mocked, and crucified so we could argue about doctrine, church policies, or theological differences? Did God permit His Son to shed His blood in the horrors of Calvary only so we could chatter in tongues to each other? Is it feasible that the terrors of the cross fell upon our Savior simply so we could argue our denominational distinctive? And most critical—did Jesus die so that we could shrink in isolation while the world outside our walls flounders in desperation, looking for a true, never-ending love? No! Jesus died so that all who believe could have a forever friendship with Him. He sent His Holy Spirit so that relationship could begin now.

In Song of Solomon we read of a lover who comes for his bride, imploring her to run away with him! This beautiful book is actually a song. In a later chapter in this book we will look at Song of Solomon through the lens of marital intimacy. But within this tender song, we find a special word to those of us hungry for intimacy with God.

Our relationship with God is often illustrated in Scripture as that of a courting couple or in the images surrounding marital intimacy. When trying to understand the full potential of life together with God, we can draw some important lessons from the young couple in Song of Solomon:

> My beloved spoke, and said to me: "Rise up, my love, my fair one, and come away. For lo, the winter is past, the rain is over and gone. The flowers appear on the earth; the time of singing has come, and the voice of the turtledove is heard in our land. The fig tree puts forth her green figs, and the vines with the tender grapes give a good smell. Rise up, my love, my fair one, and come away! O my dove, in the clefts of the rock, in the secret places of the cliff, let me see your face, let me hear your voice; for your voice is sweet, and your face is lovely."
>
> —SONG OF SOLOMON 2:10–14

She falls in love with a shepherd and finds out later when he comes for her that he is actually a king! The Book of Song of Solomon illustrates Christ's love for us. Our Lord and Lover came to us first as the Shepherd. "I am the good shepherd. The good shepherd lays down his life for the sheep" (John 10:11, NIV). We fell in love with Him as a Good Shepherd who was willing to lead us, feed us, love us, and die for us. It is an amazing picture, and honestly, difficult to comprehend how much the King of the universe loves us and desires fellowship with us. His beautiful words, leaping off the pages of Scripture, call us away from our daily responsibilities and into His arms. What keeps you from an intimate life together with God?

Chapter 5

BENEFITS TO LIVING IN AGREEMENT WITH GOD

By Ron Phillips

I HOPE YOU ARE beginning to understand the simple progression here. Our walk with God begins with a quest for Him. We must understand the barriers that prevent us from having that life with Him. Then we must identify the steps we must take in order to enjoy a life of agreement with God. In this chapter we want you to understand some of the benefits to having a life that is intimately connected to God.

Abraham discovered this and became a "spiritual insider" with God. God called him "friend." When God was about to unleash judgment on Sodom and Gomorrah, He let Abraham in on that plan:

> And the LORD said, "Shall I hide from Abraham what I am doing, since Abraham shall surely become a great

and mighty nation, and all the nations of the earth shall
be blessed in him?"

—Genesis 18:17–18

Access

The first benefit of a life together with God is access. In the
old covenant only the high priest could access the holy of
holies, which housed the divine presence of God. In the new
covenant everyone who knows Jesus has access to His presence and power. Too often, though, we act as if we seek God's
face, when honestly we seek only His hand. We try to pull at
His purse strings instead of crying out for His presence! If we
don't know the Father intimately, we will never understand
the unfathomable benefits that are available to us as insiders.

Think about your close friends and think about your social
media "friends." Your close friends know a lot more about
you than people who have "friended" you on Facebook, or
who "follow you" on Twitter or any other social network out
there. Just because they are listed as a "friend" doesn't mean
that they have true access to your life. Have those strangers
in your social network ever sat down to a meal in your home?
Do you speak to them regularly on the phone? Do you pray
together, shop together, play sports together? Have they cried
with you over the disappointments in your life? No. Despite
the unnecessary details you may give the world through your
social media accounts, those people are not insiders. They
are not with you for the real life that you are living. Real
access comes through a personal relationship. In Jesus you
have access to God!

PROVISION

You may be Donald Trump's "fan" in social media, but you do not have access to the resources available to his children. You may have access to view the public side of his life, but that is as far as your access goes. God provides for the needs of those who are close to Him, and because of that insider relationship we can begin to understand the benefits of that connection. The following passage from Numbers in the Old Testament reveals that blessing:

> And the LORD spoke to Moses, saying: "Speak to Aaron and his sons, saying, 'This is the way you shall bless the children of Israel. Say to them:
> "The LORD bless you and keep you;
> The LORD make His face shine upon you,
> And be gracious to you;
> The Lord lift up His countenance upon you,
> And give you peace."
>
> 'So they shall put My name on the children of Israel, and I will bless them.'"
> —NUMBERS 6:22–27

This blessing is full of promise. Yahweh told Moses to release this blessing through Aaron and the priestly line to all of the Jews. They were to speak God's name, which is Yahweh, the Great I Am, upon the people. His name houses unlimited blessing, immunity, protection, and God's favor and presence!

Isaiah 45 celebrated the release of Israel from bondage by the anointed leader Cyrus of Persia. Cyrus did not know that he was God's instrument to bless His people. Listen to this

first promise of material provision: "I will give you the trea-
sures of darkness and hidden riches of secret places, that you
may know that I, the LORD, who call you by your name, am
the God of Israel" (Isa. 45:3).

One of the blessings of life together with God is that we
become partakers in God's promise to provide our material
needs. When we enter His presence, Yahweh loads us with
benefits and blessing. The promise of showers of blessing
comes many times in Scripture, including this verse in Isaiah:
"Rain down, you heavens, from above, and let the skies pour
down righteousness; let the earth open, let them bring forth
salvation, and let righteousness spring up together. I, the
LORD, have created it" (45:8).

Not only does God promise to pour out salvation upon the
whole earth and maintain a plan to touch the world, but God
also begs us to pray:

> Thus says the LORD, the Holy One of Israel, and his
> Maker: "Ask Me of things to come concerning My sons;
> and concerning the work of My hands, you command Me."
> —ISAIAH 45:11

He invites us to command His blessing on all the works
of His hand. The provision of Yahweh will flow through your
prayers. He commands us to boldly make our requests. Then
Yahweh promises us the riches of the world:

> Thus says the LORD:
> "The labor of Egypt and merchandise of Cush
> And of the Sabeans, men of stature,
> Shall come over to you, and they shall be yours;
> They shall walk behind you,

They shall come over in chains;
And they shall bow down to you.
They will make supplication to you, saying,
'Surely God is in you,
And there is no other;
There is no other God.'"

—Isaiah 45:14

Covenant

We are promised, "The secret of the LORD is with those who fear Him, and He will show them His covenant" (Ps. 25:14). God wants to reveal marvelous secrets of His kingdom. Are you one of the few who will wait on Him and listen? As we bow in fear and reverence before Him, He will show us all the covenant promises made to us in Christ Jesus. The Bible is filled with mysteries that God is still fulfilling. God wants to reveal to you all that is yours in the new covenant. What did God promise through this covenant? Our covenant promises many benefits including healing, deliverance, freedom, and prosperity.

Covering

In biblical times and even today, devout Jewish men worshipping in the temple wore a covering called a *talith*, or prayer cloth. This covering was a symbol that they were spending intimate time alone with God. That is what our secret place is like—a covering. King David wrote, "He who dwells in the secret place of the Most High shall abide under the shadow of the Almighty" (Ps. 91:1). We are also to "abide" under the shadow of the Almighty. The word *abide* means "to tarry all night." It speaks of the intimacy of lovers, husband and wife, who tarry all night loving each other. Here is the divine glory covering us, loving us, and hovering protectively over us. Having entered this close relationship with Jesus by trust, we become the beneficiaries of divine covering!

PROTECTION

Like a young eagle in its mother's nest, you are safe in God's presence. His truth covers and protects you. Psalm 91 reminds us, "He shall cover you with His feathers, and under His wings you shall take refuge; His truth shall be your shield and buckler. You shall not be afraid of the terror by night, nor of the arrow that flies by day" (vv. 4–5). Night terrors are a great problem for many today, children and adults alike. Fears of the dark remain with some youngsters into their adult lives. Yet the unknown night stalkers of hell do not have a place in the lives of believers who are intimately together with God! No arrow of the wicked can penetrate the shield of faith and trust that guards the entrance to the secret place! In His presence the old fears leave. God promises, "A thousand may fall at your side, and ten thousand at your right hand; but it shall not come near you" (Ps. 91:7). While others may become victims of the enemy's attacks on their hearts and minds, you will be safe because of your close relationship to Him.

Some years ago a demented man approached me in the parking lot following a revival service. He was about to hit me when my staff assistant grabbed the man's arm. With his other hand, the staff member pushed me into the car and faced my attacker for me. That night my staff assistant was literally my shield! If we abide in this place of protection then we have Jesus and His angelic host present to step in for us.

No evil shall befall you,
Nor shall any plague come near your dwelling;
For He shall give His angels charge over you,
To keep you in all your ways.
In their hands they shall bear you up,
Lest you dash your foot against a stone.
—PSALM 91:10–12

There is just something about the name *Jesus*! His name is power, and within the folds of its protection believers can know a secret place where there is anointing, safety, and blessing—a tower of strength that keeps us from evil. Our planet has become the "killing fields" of hell, yet we can experience immunity to all these plagues. Here is a place where neither devil nor disease can disturb our walk or destroy our witness for Jesus. You see, we go in His strength! We actually carry His dwelling with us! Angels watch over our every step. "Are they not all ministering spirits sent forth to minister for those who will inherit salvation?" (Heb. 1:14).

INTIMACY

If you are going to avoid evil, you must have an intimate relationship with Jesus Christ. In just the first two verses of Psalm 91, we find four different names of God! Our Maker wants us to know His name, to be acquainted with His very character. How do you get into God's presence and abide there? Here is the golden gateway into God's presence: "I will say of the LORD, 'He is my refuge and my fortress; my God, in Him I will trust'" (Ps. 91:2). This bears repeating: God inhabits praise! When we begin to audibly confess His Word out of our mouths, when we worship His might and power, then we discover the place of intimacy with Him! We move into what the psalmist David called the secret place of the Most High, which is an open door to His presence.

INVINCIBILITY

Once you are enjoying the place of intimacy together with God, you move on to a place of invincibility. In the safety of the shadow of His presence, Psalm 91 tells us, we will escape many traps of the enemy. You discover that God will "deliver you from the snare of the fowler." In biblical times, a snare was used to catch birds or animals. This snare contained a lure. The devil sets dangerous traps for believers. But those who are walking with God, talking with Him in prayer and speaking or singing His praises, will be delivered from these traps, including deception, doubt, darkness, demonic forces, disease, disasters, and defeat. If you are listening to God's voice and walking with Him on a daily basis, it doesn't mean that disasters won't happen. It doesn't mean the disease won't come. It simply means that those things cannot stop you from enjoying the benefits of life together with God. You will not be lured into the enemy's destructive trap.

IMMUNITY

There is a difference between invincibility and immunity. *Invincibility* means you can escape evil's trap. *Immunity* means that long before it gets to your borders, you'll have spiritual insight and you will be out of the way. Millions of dollars have been spent placing tsunami warning systems into the Indian Ocean following the devastation that hit India in December 2004. These devices are ultra-sensitive, sending a split-second signal to a satellite if the ocean rises even a foot, and warning potentially affected countries within moments of detection.[1] This depicts the power of our connection with God. His warning system gives us notice and prompting long before evil can come to hinder our path!

In the historic home of John Wesley, the great Methodist minister, there is a very small upstairs room. This was his prayer room, which he used daily at 4:00 a.m.[2] No wonder so many hymns, so much ministry, and so much anointing flowed out of Wesley. He had an appointment with God at 4:30 each morning! As a result, this promise was his: "Because you have made the LORD, who is my refuge, even the Most High, your dwelling place, No evil shall befall you, nor shall any plague come near your dwelling" (Ps. 91:9–10).

INCREASE

Another benefit of a life lived in agreement with God is increase. This is a wonderful promise from God: "'Because he loves me,' says the LORD, 'I will rescue him; I will protect him, for he acknowledges my name'" (Ps. 91:14, NIV). When we go after God as an ardent lover, when we pursue Him with passion, God promises to increase every area of our lives. To know His name is to be called by His name. Thus, as we shall see, the family name releases our inheritance.

INHERITANCE

In the Old Testament, a person's name was more than simply a tag. Rather, it represented the character, virtue, family essence, and resources of an individual. When we whisper the name "Jesus," we are uttering the mightiest, most majestic name of all time; the magnum opus of all titles is given to the Almighty!

David Kaplan was a Chicago sports personality who

decided his family name was worth more than money. Dallas Mavericks owner Mark Cuban asked the sportscaster to consider changing his name to "Dallas Maverick." Cuban offered $50,000 to Kaplan if he would do it! Kaplan balked, so Cuban upped the offer to $100,0000, plus another $100,000 to go to Kaplan's favorite charity, and added that Kaplan would have to adopt the name change for only one year.[3] What would you do? Kaplan decided to decline the lucrative offer. A *Chicago Tribune* article quoted him explaining, "My name is my birthright. I'd like to preserve my integrity and credibility."[4]

Our loving God established His name in the earth, a name above all names! As we approach the secret place, it is a joy to speak the name of Jesus and experience the wonder of the mighty character of the Lord! In Matthew 16, Jesus laid the foundational truth upon which He would assemble His people into the body and family we call the church. It is interesting that Jesus began this lesson to His own insiders by asking them to tell Him His name. He asked them, "Who do you say that I am?" (Matt. 16:15).

This is the essential question of the Christian life, the only question on the final exam of Christian possibility! If we do not know His name, we will not be able to abide in Him and do His work as sons and daughters. How can we ever know who we are if we do not know who He is? After spending three years with His disciples Jesus wanted to know their perception of Him. Peter got an A+ for his answer:

> Simon Peter answered and said, "You are the Christ, the Son of the living God." Jesus answered and said to him, "Blessed are you, Simon Bar-Jonah, for flesh and blood has not revealed this to you, but My Father who is in heaven. And I also say to you that you are Peter, and on

this rock I will build My church, and the gates of Hades
shall not prevail against it."
—MATTHEW 16:16–18

Simon Peter came to know Jesus's name the same way we
can know it—by divine revelation. The Holy Spirit revealed
that the fullness of God permanently dwelt in Jesus. If we
have a true understanding of His name, God will build His
church on that knowledge. There is significance in knowing
God's name. "Knowing" means much more than simply
having information in your brain; rather, it refers to the
closest possible intimacy. To know God's name is to be an
intimate who has learned all the facets and nuances of His
character. The name of Jesus encompasses so much! As we
observed in Psalm 91:14, we must acknowledge His name.
He is:

- *Yahweh*—the Great I Am

- *Jireh*—my Provider

- *Tsidkenu*—my Righteousness

- *Rophe*—my Healer

- *Rohi*—my Shepherd

- *Nissi*—my Leader and Lover

- *Shalom*—my Peace

- *Shammah*—my Companion

Yes, He is also our Christ, the Anointed One, and the
Messiah of the world. He is Wonderful! He is our Lord! He is
before the beginning and after the end! He is the unceasing

song of David resounding across time and all of creation! He is the Ever-Shining Star that will never fade. It is Jesus's scarred hands that invite us to this intimate life, His shining face that welcomes us in. Here, we whisper His name, Jesus, and find ourselves abiding in the Almighty, overwhelmed with the promise and blessing of His presence!

KEYS

When we get inside the secret place, the name of Jesus releases the keys to the kingdom. Everything we need is now available. He has given us the means to unlock every resource needed to finish the work He has called us to do. From shortage to abundance, from weakness to strength, and from defeat to victory: all of these blessings flow to us in His presence. I want you to see three important keys that you are handed by the Lord that will help you open every roadblock along your journey to an intimate life together with God.

1. Praise and worship

> To the angel of the church in Philadelphia write:
> "These are the words of him who is holy and true, who holds the key of David. What he opens no one can shut, and what he shuts no one can open."
> —REVELATION 3:7, NIV

Worship opens up kingdom authority and access permanently.

2. Kingdom resources

> "I will place on his shoulder the key to the house of David; what he opens no one can shut."
> —ISAIAH 22:22, NIV

Kingdom resources are available directly from the King!

3. Death and hell—the good news of Jesus

> "I am the Living One; I was dead, and behold I am alive for ever and ever! And I hold the keys of death and Hades."
> —REVELATION 1:18, NIV

Because Jesus died and came to life again, conquering our sin debt and eternal punishment, we forever hold the key to eternal life through Jesus!

Everything flows to those who know His name!

> "I will give you the keys of the kingdom of heaven; and whatever you bind on earth shall have been bound in heaven, and whatever you loose on earth shall have been loosed in heaven."
> —MATTHEW 16:19, NAS

What an exciting promise, to know that we will see what God is doing in heaven and declare it bound or loosed on earth! Our prayers, instead of hit or miss, become informed. In His presence, we discover what He is saying and doing, and by the prayer of faith, move it to earth. Psalm 91:14–16 reveals more clear promises to those who dwell in His presence, love His name, and have no desire but to know Him better.

- *I will deliver him…*

  This means the enemy will never hold you in sin's spiritual prison!

- *I will set him on high…*

  God will take care of your reputation. So let promotion come from the Lord.

- *He shall call upon Me, and I will answer…*

  God will always answer your prayers.

- *I will be with him in trouble…*

  This promise assures us we will never face anything alone! In Matthew 28:20, Jesus said: "Lo, I am with you always, even to the end of the age."

- *I will honor him…*

  Only the applause of heaven really matters. His "well done" is enough.

- *With long life I will satisfy him…*

  A satisfied, full, and overflowing life is found in a life enjoyed together with God!

- *I will show him My salvation.*

  The word for salvation in this passage is *Yeshua*, which is Hebrew for Jesus! So, the best promise is saved for last—God will show us Jesus! To see Jesus is the beginning and end of everything.

There are tremendous benefits awaiting you in the secret place with God. Your time spent seeking Him will not be in vain! Those who seek Him will hear His voice. God will reveal His riches to you as you get alone with Him and seek His face. Once there, tell your heavenly Father what you need. Is the gas tank of your life on empty? His provision is abundant and miraculous. In His service, at the feet of Jesus, you will find the Lord to be everything you need!

Chapter 6

HINDRANCES TO LIVING IN AGREEMENT WITH GOD

By Ron Phillips

G OD'S INTEREST IN us is intense and personal. Like the king in Song of Solomon, the heavenly Father comes "leaping upon the mountains, skipping upon the hills," overtaking every barrier to life lived in agreement with Him (Song of Sol. 2:8). Think of those mountains as the challenges that loom before each of us, those things that seem impossible to get through. All of the difficulties that are roadblocks or detours on your journey are no match for the resolve of our Lord.

WALLS

Just when the journey seems too difficult, Jesus gladly comes to our aid. He draws near, and the enemy presents new problems to try to block His aid. Jesus reminds us of His help in the middle of difficulty: "These things I have spoken to you, that in Me you may have peace. In the world you will have tribulation; but be of good cheer, I have overcome the world" (John 16:33).

So often our Lord cannot get to us because of the walls *we* have erected. These walls are sin, in the form of complacency, preoccupation, fear, prayerlessness, and pride. These walls can become strongholds that give the enemy access. The Father's voice calls to us across all barriers and boundaries to life together. "Rise up, my love, my fair one, and come away" (Song of Sol. 2:10). You see, we have a choice to make. We can stay where we are in our indecision, or take the risk and move forward to enjoy life together with God.

Indecision

Through the ages, men and women have found themselves floundering, in over their heads in the course of life. When you don't know what to do, it is natural to look around for somewhere safe where the trouble and turbulence cannot touch you. Like us, the prophet Elijah knew what it was to wish for a safe escape! He had obeyed God and stood up to the treacherous King Ahab, delivering the unpopular news that a severe famine was to hit the land. Elijah no doubt feared for his life after speaking such a dramatic, prophetic word, but God made provision for him. First Kings 17:3–4 states: "Get away from here and turn eastward, and hide by the Brook Cherith, which flows into the Jordan. And it will be that you shall drink from the brook, and I have commanded the ravens to feed you there."

Since Eden, all sons and daughters of Adam have been trying to get beyond the barriers, trying to discover the place where God will meet them. They hope for a better life, a greater reality, deeper meaning, or more purpose in life. The children of Israel journeyed across a wilderness for forty years looking for a new life with God. Abraham left a suburban home in the city of Ur to live in a tent because he was looking for the place where God could be found. David found a deeper life with God on the side of the hill while tending sheep, enjoying green pastures and still waters. Each of these Bible characters was longing for a better life together with God, but they never would have found that place if they had allowed indecision to paralyze them.

Indecision keeps you from taking the first step. Indecision robs you of intimacy with God. Indecision keeps you bogged down in the clutter of daily living, bound by life's circumstances. Although each of these characters found God when in a certain place, life together with God is not necessarily referring to a specific geographical location that you can pin on the maps app on your smartphone. The supernatural presence of God breaks through heaven and into your life when you take the first step toward God by faith. Are you ready to get past indecision?

PREOCCUPATION

Verse 3 goes on to say, "Get away from here and turn *eastward*" (emphasis added). The word *eastward* in Deuteronomy 33:27 reads: "The eternal God is your refuge, and underneath are the everlasting arms; He will thrust out the enemy from before you, and will say, 'Destroy!'"

That word *eternal* in this verse is the same word translated *eastward* in 1 Kings 17:3. You need to realize that preoccupation will keep you from the place where your heart turns toward the eternal! *East* is the place in Scripture where the eternal God is, the place where the everlasting arms are. The *eastward* God—the *eternal* God—is your refuge! From that place He will say to the enemy, "You are finished."

God told Elijah to "hide by the brook." It was in this private time that God met him personally. Preoccupation will sabotage your quiet moments with the Father and prevent you from discovering the secret of the hidden life together with God.

A man asked me what resources I use to write my sermons. "Where do you get your ideas?" he asked.

I replied, "It's true that I have a vast library, and I've read most of the books. I have computer aids that are valuable tools. However, I prepare my messages by looking at every word that proceeds out of the mouth of God! Many times, on Saturday especially, I'll hear God calling me down to meet Him in the small study in the basement of my home. My wife, Paulette, understands this because she also hears God calling her at five o'clock in the morning! When I get up, more than likely I'll find her on the porch weeping with an open Bible. If it is winter, I'll find her sitting by the gas logs. That is where she regularly finds time together with God."

Colossians 3:3 says that you are dead and "your life is hidden with Christ in God." There is a hidden life with God. Psalm 91 calls it the secret place of the Most High. There is a place only you can go with God. Deuteronomy 29:29 says, "The secret things belong to the LORD our God, but those things which are revealed belong to us." The Hebrew word for *"secret"* has the same meaning as the Greek word translated "hide" in Colossians 3:3. There is a place where God will whisper His secrets in your ear. There is a place where the things unknown can be revealed to your heart and your soul.

Are you allowing preoccupation to rob you of the secret to intimate time together with God?

There is another Old Testament character who was preoccupied. His name, Jacob, means "wheeler dealer." He was shrewd and crafty, using his skill to steal his own brother's blessing and birthright. His life was a constant chase, with Yahweh in hot pursuit of His fleeing child. Jacob was always in a hurry. If you look at his early life, it resembles a spiritual yo-yo. On one life-changing journey, Jacob turned aside to rest from his travels, using a stone for a pillow. As he slept, he had visions of stairs leading to heaven! In that supernatural encounter, Yahweh promised Jacob manifold blessings.

> Then he dreamed, and behold, a ladder was set up on the earth, and its top reached to heaven; and there the angels of God were ascending and descending on it. And behold, the LORD stood above it and said: "I am the LORD God of Abraham your father and the God of Isaac; the land on which you lie I will give to you and your descendants. Also your descendants shall be as the dust of the earth; you shall spread abroad to the west and the east, to the north and the south; and in you and in your seed all the families of the earth shall be blessed."
>
> —GENESIS 28:12–14

Despite this important experience, Jacob did not stop his hurried lifestyle. Like most of us, he had a schedule, appointments, and plan of his own. And so, Yahweh again sought his attention, this time literally wrestling him to the ground, crippling him in order to bless him (Gen. 32:24–32). This second face-to-face encounter resulted in Jacob receiving a new name, Israel, which means "prince of God."

Preoccupation had to be broken in the busy and distracted Jacob.

Unbelievably Israel slipped back to his old "Jacob" patterns! Like so many of us, he refused to embrace life together with God. Before long Jacob's family faced disaster. His daughter was raped, and his sons killed hundreds of young men. God again summoned Jacob in response to this horrific situation. Then God said to Jacob, "Arise, go up to Bethel and dwell there; and make an altar there to God, who appeared to you when you fled from the face of Esau your brother" (Gen. 35:1). Finally, Jacob told his household and all who were with him to put away the foreign gods, purify themselves, and go up to Bethel. He built an altar there and called it El Bethel, because it was the place where God appeared to him when he fled from the face of his brother.

There is an urgent and comforting lesson in this choice. Yes, indeed, the quest for life together with God is made possible through the awesome gift of God's grace. Grace is God's favor for the disfavored! Grace allows the Jacobs of today to climb to the status of Israel and become "princes of God." You won't sit on a literal throne over a literal kingdom, but yes, all that Jacob was promised is ours as well, male or female. But we have to put away preoccupation, and stop running, wrestling, and wandering about life aimlessly. We have access to God's presence. We can ascend the hill of the Lord. He has invited us to come home.

When I was in seminary, I remember facing a particularly trying time of deep discouragement. A friend grabbed me and said, "Ron, let's pray!" We were in the hallway at the time, so he looked around for a more private spot and steered me under the staircase. As he began to pray I felt the Holy Spirit begin to lift me out of my despair. That place under those apartment stairs became a secret place of prayer where God was able to shape my life.

The Lord is very near. Like Jacob, you may be running hard in life. Don't be alarmed; the Lord is as near as your breath. In your secret place, He will show up, angels will operate, His Word will be clear, and His love will wash you. He is waiting for you, calling you to that rendezvous underneath His staircase. Jacob ran headlong into God. Are you too busy, too preoccupied, and in too big of a hurry to enjoy life together with God?

FEAR

Fear is a strong barrier to living and enjoying life with God. How many times have you allowed fear to limit your potential, negate your God-given promise, or literally paralyze you in the face of danger? Life together with God is to be lived in freedom. Freedom from fear is a life free of torments. Torments come literally through people and situations. When the tsunami hit off the coast of Japan, fear ripped through the coastal villages, then the entire country as the nuclear plant was compromised.

Fear paralyzed New York City and the onlooking world on 9/11 when terrorists tried to demoralize the United States of America by their acts of terrorism against innocent people and the economic, military, and governmental centers of our nation. Those types of fears are understandable in the middle of crisis. But fear also comes by way of thoughts the enemy plants in our minds. These thoughts, if allowed to have free rein in our thinking, bring fear and will torment our lives.

King David understood the value of life together with God,

and he found strength to face his fears in the secret place as a shepherd boy out on the hillside. Imagine the shadows and dangers he faced alone in the dark night tending sheep. Read Psalm 17:8–9 carefully: "Keep me as the apple of Your eye; hide me under the shadow of Your wings, from the wicked who oppress me, from my deadly enemies who surround me." When you are under attack, there is a hiding place you can run to and find safety. King David also wrote in Psalm 27:5, "For in the time of trouble He shall hide me in His pavilion; in the secret place of His tabernacle He shall hide me; He shall set me high upon a rock."

In the same way, God looked at Elijah when everyone wanted to kill him, when the drought had come, when everything was wrong, and said, "Hide yourself." When the attacks of the enemy and the voices of darkness come against you, take comfort in the hiding place. Our heavenly Father will pick you up, comfort you, wash you clean again in His blood, and strengthen you. You may have been down, but He will set you on the course with Him if you will abandon fear and allow the Holy Spirit to remove the preoccupation over your circumstances.

REJECTION

One of the most difficult barriers to life with God is rejection. Most of us feel rejected by other people, and a result some even feel rejected by God. When we reject God's love and provision, we are miles away from life together with God. When life became difficult for the prophet Elijah, he fled to the Brook Cherith. Now, at the brook he is in a solitary place with God. Some scholars have researched this place and have been puzzled by the realization that there is no record of an actual "Brook Cherith." But a clue comes when we uncover what the word *Cherith* means. In Genesis 15:18, God came to Abram and said, "I want to cut a covenant with you." *Cherith Berith* in Hebrew means to cut a covenant. So, God spoke to Elijah, saying, "Go to the brook where I cut a covenant." From these clues, I believe that the brook was the Jabath, where Jacob wrestled with the angel. The Jabath was a rushing stream and a refreshing haven. If you ride down the West Bank in Israel, you can look across the Jordan River and see Mount Gilead, the fertile area where Elijah hid himself. It's still fertile! There is still a river flowing.

You may say you are dry, failing of hope, feeling rejected and alone. It is time to remember that there is water coming off a mountain! A river is flowing from Calvary, all the way down into your life! The people wanted to kill him, but Elijah found God's love to be refreshing waters of covenant. Isn't that where our hearts should desire to go? There is a secret and hidden life together with God. It is real, and not just something that great men and women of God from ages ago experienced, but a covenant that can be yours now!

Legalism

Like Elijah, we have to choose to receive God's covenant with us or reject it. God told him in 1 Kings 17:4, "And it will be that you shall drink from the brook, and I have commanded the ravens to feed you there." It is significant that God chose ravens to be the delivery agents. Basically, the raven was a buzzard! That particular bird mauled the sick and dying and was considered unclean according to the laws given to Israel. Yet all the food that Elijah received from God for several months was brought to him by this dirty bird!

God looked at his number one prophet, Elijah, a man who was under the law, and God basically said, "If you think it's going to be like it's always been, you are wrong. I'm going to break the spirit of legalism." If Elijah had rejected God's provision rather than change, he would have died in the famine. Of course, not only did Elijah have to change, but God had to redirect the nature of the raven as well! By nature, ravens scavenge and eat meat—they don't carry it to someone else!

Even today God can change the hearts of our enemies in order to keep covenant with us! Are you willing to allow God to change your nature and break you free from your traditional thought processes if they are limiting you from having and becoming all that God wants for you to experience in your relationship with Him? Take a few minutes to think about those limiting factors in your life. Ask God to remove the barriers, and then cooperate with Him. Take a step toward life together with Him.

Chapter 7

FIRST STEPS WITH GOD

By Ron Phillips

T HE MOVIE *THELMA & Louise* presented a parable of human drama and tragedy. In a desire to flee from abuse and violence, these two women ran from their past. Pursued by authorities, the women let their behavior escalate from harmless pranks into criminal acts. The movie ends with the two women hurtling to their deaths as they drive their car over the edge of the Grand Canyon. Their attempts to run from the past and control their future culminated in the ultimate end for both of them. Thelma and Louise chose a path that took them over the edge, literally![1]

Real-life stories of tragedy fill the pages of our family trees, make headlines in our news feeds, and rock our communities and yes, even our churches. These two fictional characters never took the first and most important step that everyone must take if they want to overcome their past and live a fulfilled life.

Receiving Forgiveness

If we are ever going to know lasting peace and how to properly respond to the difficulties of life, we must embrace the forgiveness that can be found only in Jesus Christ. He was despised, rejected, lied about, and tempted in every way that we are tempted, but He remained blameless so that He could be the substitute for the sentence of guilt that each of us deserves to pay for our sin. Receiving forgiveness is the first step toward life together with God. There is no option on this first step. Without Jesus, there is no possible way to have a life together with God.

One of the most relatable Old Testament examples of someone who experienced the forgiveness of God is David. As a little boy David was different than others. He was odd in appearance compared to most other Israelites. In a dark-eyed, dark-skinned culture, he had "bright eyes" and was "ruddy, and of a fair countenance" (1 Sam. 17:42, kjv). David—the blue-eyed, pale-skinned redhead! David's family tried to hide him. When the prophet Samuel showed up at the house of Jesse to anoint the second king of Israel, Jesse didn't mention his youngest son, David, at first. David the "different" one was safely hidden in the field taking care of the sheep. Despite this environment of prejudice and sibling angst, David had learned that he was never alone. As a shepherd, he had discovered out on the hillside that, "The Lord is my shepherd" (Ps. 23:1). That Shepherd protected and forgave him throughout his life, despite his many failures.

SURRENDER

Most of us who have embraced God's forgiveness still try to take control of our lives, even after that first step. Instead of growing more passionately in love with Jesus, we become practical and predictable. Soon our hot hearts cool to a lukewarm state that is tasteless and safely offends no one. We find people like Mary of Bethany, who weep and wash Jesus's feet with their tears, embarrassingly emotional. Shepherds like David who whirl and dance and play instruments to express their love to the Lord are relegated to the lonely hillside. Sadly, we now treat faith in Jesus as something to fit neatly into our day planners, primarily an hour or two on Sunday. During the rest of our week, we are in pursuit of our own interests. You might call this a "high-speed race to nowhere"! We must surrender control of our lives to the Lord and His desire for us to release a life of running, wrestling, and failing, and to grab hold of a life that has wings!

STILLNESS

A life together with God embraces forgiveness, surrenders, and practices stillness. This step is hit or miss for most believers. We are summoned to be alone with God so that we can communicate with Him. We are summoned to the cleft of the Rock, a high and holy place.

Just as the holy of holies in the tabernacle housed the presence of God, we are summoned to a personal audience with Jesus. Psalm 24:3–6 speaks to those who crave the awesome presence of Jesus:

Who may ascend into the hill of the LORD?
Or who may stand in His holy place?
He who has clean hands and a pure heart,
Who has not lifted up his soul to an idol,
Nor sworn deceitfully.
He shall receive blessing from the LORD,
And righteousness from the God of his salvation.
This *is* Jacob, the generation of those who seek Him,
Who seek Your face.

David became a lover of the Lord Jesus out in those fields. God became the greatest desire of his young heart! Long evenings of solitude under the starry heavens taught David that he was never alone! What may have appeared to be a crude country life was far more. Every star above his head sang of the love of God. In the darkness of night, David's soul glowed with the light of God's presence. "The LORD is my light and my salvation; whom shall I fear? The LORD is the strength of my life; of whom shall I be afraid?" (Ps. 27:1). When David trudged up the hills of Judea, the simple trek was transformed by the presence of God. "I will lift up my eyes to the hills—from whence comes my help?" (Ps. 121:1). Suddenly, his trail upward became a pilgrim journey into the secret place! Every outcropping of rock became the "shadow of the Almighty." Even gurgling streams carried echoes of heaven. David practiced the presence of God and learned the skills of a leader and shepherd as he worshipped and communed with Jehovah.

His most famous work, Psalm 23, sums up David's extraordinary wilderness experience with God. David's intimacy with his Creator propelled him forward to courageous leadership and fame. His rock-solid assurance of God's faithfulness sent him to fell Goliath, protected him from Saul's fury, elevated him to leadership, attracted others to follow him, and finally took him to the throne. David knew God as Lord, Yahweh, the Great I Am, and the God of covenant! He understood God was the Shepherd of Israel, the Provider, and his Protector. This future king may have been walking in the wilderness, but he inhabited the house of God!

WORSHIP

David learned that God's presence was brought on by praising God and entering into worship. Worship is the next step toward life together with God. As David cared for his sheep, he learned to conquer fear. He faced and killed both a lion and a bear while tending those sheep. Even as he stood guard over his flock, he came to understand that God was close by his side. When your problems rise up before you like a Goliath, what can you do? You can worship and have faith in God! Your worship will lift you above that which had towered over you. As you sing and commune with God, you enter a place of intimate fellowship.

Like David, you may come from a dysfunctional family. You may be different from the rest of your relatives and even feel like an outcast. Take heart! You can turn your solitude into a sanctuary and turn your loneliness into life! Remember, David received the anointing of God to lead the people, different as he was. Goliath could not kill him. The jealous King Saul could not destroy him. The Philistines could not buy him off. Hell could not stop him. Even sin could not finish him, for he knew the power of that first step—God's forgiveness.

David sang out to the God of his salvation not to gain anything for himself—he didn't want wealth, titles, or land. His whole desire was to know the heart of God. He wrote:

One thing I have desired of the LORD,
That will I seek:
That I may dwell in the house of the LORD
All the days of my life,
To behold the beauty of the LORD,
And to inquire in His temple.
For in the time of trouble
He shall hide me in His pavilion;
In the secret place of His tabernacle
He shall hide me;
He shall set me high upon a rock.
And now my head shall be lifted up above my enemies
    all around me;
Therefore I will offer sacrifices of joy in His tabernacle;
I will sing, yes, I will sing praises to the LORD.
Hear, O LORD, when I cry with my voice!
Have mercy also upon me, and answer me.
When You said, "Seek My face,"
My heart said to You, "Your face, LORD, I will seek."
Do not hide Your face from me;
Do not turn Your servant away in anger;
You have been my help;
Do not leave me nor forsake me,
O God of my salvation.

—PSALM 27:4–9

At this point, no temple had been built, so in this psalm he isn't referring to traditional church attendance as you may first think. Here David refers to the private hours spent in the secret place worshipping God. David was seeking God's presence! David longed to gaze on the beauty of the Lord and live in His presence.

One summer I learned an important lesson about the importance of God's response to our worship. The hot

Nigerian sun beat down upon our team as we prepared to leave for the airport. I had been in Africa for a preaching crusade, and though the time had come to leave our host pastor, we took a moment to pray and rejoice with Dr. Ezeh before departing. The prayers for provision for our journey still rang in our ears as we walked into the local airport only to discover in shock that our flight to Lagos had been cancelled! This news had serious implications: if we did not make it to Lagos that very day, we would miss our flight out of Africa, and our return to the United States would be delayed four days until the next available outbound flight! Some quick scrambling and calculating revealed that our only hope was to make a mad three-and-a-half-hour dash to catch a different flight from the airport in Port Harcourt, but we had to hustle to find appropriate vehicles and leave immediately, as we had only a fifteen-minute time margin! The situation was made even more complicated by the fact that gasoline was scarce in Nigeria at the time. A two-week shutdown of the refineries had left the nation in the grip of a fuel shortage. Many gas stations were closed or were rationing fuel. An hour into our drive, I noticed that the gas gauge in our borrowed vehicle registered below empty. I leaned forward and asked our Nigerian driver, Brother A. G. Bright, if his fuel gauge was broken. "No, my brother," he answered, "but God will provide, for we prayed for mercy on this journey. Also, you and Dr. Ezeh are God's men. He will surely see us through."

It is difficult to admit, but my faithless soul was not comforted. I immediately had visions of our team stranded with our vehicles in the middle of the sweltering Nigerian jungle! I could imagine rebels and robbers taking us captive! Suddenly my driver began to sing praises to God. Others in the car joined in, but still I fretted, sure that any second I would hear the car motor grind to a halt. After another hour of driving we came upon a crossroads, and a gas station stood at the intersection. As we pulled in, we could see that it was open for business! In fact, we soon found out that the station had been closed for a week—so the proprietor's supply was not exhausted—and actually had just reopened as we pulled up! A smiling A. G. Bright looked at me and said, "See, Pastor Phillips? God always takes care of His servants. You are in favor with God!" What a powerful lesson! Again I learned that God responds to a faithful man's passionate praise, not to my fretful desperation. God is looking for some worshippers who are ready to press on for more.

PRAYER

Worship and prayer go hand in hand. David prayed to the living God. He wanted protection and immunity from his enemies. "For in the time of trouble He shall hide me in His pavilion; in the secret place of His tabernacle He shall hide me; He shall set me high upon a rock" (Ps. 27:5). In times of trouble David prayed and the Lord lifted him above those who would destroy him. David sought the face of God. David was passionately obsessed with knowing God.

God's face turned toward a person signaled unparalleled blessing and power. Even in the time of failure and sin, David fled to the Lord. After his affair with Bathsheba, the resulting fallout of her pregnancy, and the ordered death of her husband, Uriah, David fled to the Lord. Both Psalm 32 and Psalm 51 were songs written by a broken and repentant David, prayers confessing his sins to God. His appeal for "tender mercies" grabbed the heart of God, and David was forgiven and restored.

Running headlong into the realization of God's amazing love is a transforming event! Author and former Franciscan monk Brennan Manning recalls a powerful encounter with the Lord at the end of a private spiritual retreat:

> Jesus removed the shroud of perfectionistic performance and now, forgiven and free, I ran home. For I knew that I *knew* Someone was there for me. Gripped in the depth of my soul, tears streaming down my cheeks, I internalized and finally felt all the words I have written and spoken about stubborn, unrelenting Love. That morning I understood that the words are but straw compared to the Reality.
>
> I leaped from simply being the teacher of God's love to becoming Abba's delight. I said good-bye to feeling frightened and said shalom to feeling safe.[2]

As we take steps toward life together with God, we discover that there is forgiveness for those who fail. In the honesty of confession, we find a passageway to His presence. His presence removes the fear and ushers in peace.

There is much about God we do not know. But God wants to reveal Himself and His plan to those who are willing to be His intimate friends. "The secret things belong to the LORD our God, but those things which are revealed belong to us and to our children forever, that we may do all the words of this law" (Deut. 29:29). God reveals deeper truth to those who will discipline themselves to a life together with God in prayer.

Where is the company of men and women who are willing

to take the necessary first steps that lead to an intimate life together with God? Is God calling you to the army of intercessors who can plead the cause of lost humanity to the Father?

Chapter 8

SUFFERING AND WAITING: TWO SEASONS OF LIFE THAT MOVE YOU CLOSER TO GOD

By Ron Phillips

BEFORE YOU DECIDE to skip this chapter completely—after all, most people want to avoid suffering if possible—let me encourage you to keep reading. The truth is that despite the benefits that we have just explored in the previous chapter, seasons of suffering and waiting on God happen in every life, including in the lives of those who follow God.

I can honestly say that "suffering with Him, sharing in His death" has allowed me to experience a "resurrection" of His life in me time and time again (Phil. 3:7–11). One especially difficult season for my entire family began during an ordinary but rainy drive to work for my wife, Paulette.

She was en route to the high school where she taught English. When she pulled back out onto the highway after stopping for gas, the poor driving conditions contributed to a head-on collision that destroyed her car and almost took her life.

The phone rang as I stepped out of the shower. As I picked up the receiver, I heard the voice on the other end say, "Mr. Phillips, your wife, Paulette, has been in a little fender bender." I dressed quickly and jumped in the car.

As I crested a hill on the main highway, I was unprepared for what I saw. Through the rain, I spotted my wife's little convertible, now a twisted mass of metal! An ambulance stood waiting, and workers were trying to free Paulette from the wreckage. The smell of gasoline was heavy in the air. I tried to get close to the car but was held back by emergency workers. I was frustrated and felt helpless knowing she must be desperately hurt and I was unable to offer comfort. However, God had provided someone at the scene to do that for me. A fireman, at the risk of his own life because of the potential for an explosion, removed a window from the car and climbed in next to Paulette. He covered her with an asbestos blanket, held on to her, and spoke life into her. It was his job to watch her carefully and keep her talking to be sure she wasn't falling into deep shock.

Twenty-five agonizing minutes passed before the firemen and the Jaws of Life freed her from the car. And we didn't know it then, but it would be six months before her crumpled body would allow her to return to a normal life.

As I ran to Paulette's side while they hurried her stretcher toward the ambulance, I remember clearly hearing her say, "Thank You, Lord!" I know that in the midst of that tragedy, God was there, and He provided a wonderful young Christian fireman whose presence comforted my wife in that dark hour.

His heroic presence was the touch of God. She felt carried in the Father's arms. Paulette returned home from the hospital after two weeks, but life at home was difficult. We had to rely on our extended family, our amazing church family, and heavily on the Lord to carry us through each day.

When tragedy strikes, we find ourselves in need of the assurance of God's presence more than ever before. To that point in my life, I never needed the Lord more than I did in those first hours and days following her wreck. It is no coincidence that our ascent into the most secret place with God can occur during times of great heartache and tragedy. Tears have a way of driving us from ourselves and into His arms. Who hasn't cried out in the dark night of the soul for comfort that can only come from Jesus? Expect to find the pathway to His presence stained with the tears of thousands of heartbroken saints before you.

Isaiah, the court prophet, cousin, and confidant to King Uzziah, thought he had it all. His cousin king, although a leper, had given the nation peace and hope. Isaiah's own ministry was one that sternly laid down the law to God's wayward people. He had angered them, calling them stubborn, ungrateful children, and even went as far as to compare them to "rotten, stinking grapes"! (See Isaiah 5:4.) Surely God was pleased with Isaiah's obedience in ministry. He surely had the ear and heart of his cousin, King Uzziah.

Isaiah is like many of us. When you read the first five chapters of Isaiah, though inspired, you feel that something is missing in his life. There is a lack of hope and only a vague hint of what God is actually up to. Isaiah 6 gives us the turning point—an amazing "alone" experience with God that is vivid and clear.

After Isaiah's dear cousin died suddenly, Isaiah felt his life collapsing. The hope that had sustained him and the promise of ministry in a peaceful Jerusalem that kept his eyes looking ahead seemed to evaporate. Tragedy is like that. Normally, it will either drive us to God or cause us to run away from Him. But Isaiah made the boldest decision any prophet ever made. He decided to charge into God's presence! Isaiah turned purposefully toward the temple of Solomon, the three-room structure that housed God's presence. Beyond the outer court, beyond the candlelit holy place, Isaiah knew there hung a thick veil. Beyond that veil, God promised to be present. However, the rules were clear—only the high priest could step behind the veil; anyone else would be struck down by God! Even the high priest could only enter the holy of holies once a year!

Isaiah came to the place of absolute self-abandonment, just as each of us must approach God. Death no longer mattered to Isaiah. He pushed his way past quiet worshippers and astounded priests to get to God. Isaiah needed help and hope, and had come to the end of his own resources. He was now a candidate for a miracle. He pressed past the veil into the holy of holies. The fearful protesters behind Isaiah no doubt backed away in fear, certain that this crazed man was walking straight into death.

There in the holy of holies, lit by only the Shekinah glory of God, Isaiah did die, in a sense. He died to himself and all of his own ambitions! In this bold step, I believe Isaiah gave up on Isaiah! He met Yahweh, and nothing else mattered. God was in that place, high and lifted up, with His unmatched glory trailing behind Him like the train of royal robes billowing behind a sovereign. Angelic worshippers surrounded the throne crying, "Holy!" The place shook with the voice of the angels. Isaiah 6:1–4 paints a vivid picture of the scene that Isaiah saw when he stepped inside the holy of holies:

> In the year that King Uzziah died, I saw the Lord sitting on a throne, high and lifted up, and the train of His robe filled the temple. Above it stood seraphim; each one had six wings: with two he covered his face, with two he covered his feet, and with two he flew. And one cried to another and said: "Holy, holy, holy is the LORD of hosts; the whole earth is full of His glory!" And the posts of the door were shaken by the voice of him who cried out, and the house was filled with smoke.

At that moment, Isaiah had no choice but to die to his flesh and ambitions. "Woe is me..." he cried, in an expression that could be also translated, "I am doomed!" He understood that even his own mouth, the mouth of a man of God, was unclean. Angels brought cleansing fire to touch his preaching lips, and his life was transformed. Soon he heard the voice of God crying for volunteers to carry His message. "Here am I, send me" (Isa. 6:5–8) cried the transformed Isaiah.

No man can see the Lord and continue living like nothing ever happened! No, the old life will be burned away and a new life will begin. Isaiah stormed into God's presence in the middle of his pain because he needed answers, comfort, and help. The New Testament puts it this way:

> I have been crucified with Christ; it is no longer I who live, but Christ lives in me; and the life which I now live in the flesh I live by faith in the Son of God, who loved me and gave Himself for me.
>
> —GALATIANS 2:20

And those who are Christ's have crucified the flesh with its passions and desires.

—GALATIANS 5:24

But God forbid that I should boast except in the cross of our Lord Jesus Christ, by whom the world has been crucified to me, and I to the world.

—GALATIANS 6:14

In the secret place of God, we come to the end of ourselves. We come as a bride to take on Jesus's name and nature. When we are willing to die daily, Jesus says to us:

"If anyone desires to come after Me, let him deny himself, and take up his cross daily, and follow Me. For whoever desires to save his life will lose it, but whoever loses his life for My sake will save it."

—LUKE 9:23–24

TRANSFORMED

To discover what happened to him after his life-transforming experience, just read through the rest of the pages of Isaiah's book. He could finally see beyond this earth and beyond time into the purposes of God. New revelation began to pour from his life, with prophecies that had eternal significance and weighty authority:

- A virgin-born King was coming—"call His name Immanuel" (Isa. 7:14)

- He would be God come to earth—"the government will be upon His shoulders" (Isa. 9:6)

- He would be wonderful!—(Isa. 9:6)

- He would die for His people—"He was wounded for our transgressions....He was led as a lamb to the slaughter" (Isa. 53:5, 7)

"Woe Is Me..."

They tell me that it took several attempts and an extra day to remove me from the ventilator following my emergency bypass surgery back in April of 2012. I remember waking and feeling as if I was choking to death. Knowing now about the struggle for my lungs to take over on their own, I'm certain that this experience occurred during one of those attempts.

As I struggled to breathe I heard the devil say, "I'm going to kill you. You're never going to wake up. And if you do they're going to tell you that the surgery was not successful and there is nothing else they can do for you."

Then suddenly I heard another voice. I believe it was the voice of my angel, Noble, which had visited me in my home exactly one year before. I heard him say, "That is a lie. You will live and not die!"

Almost immediately my vision, which had been black and white, transformed into full color, and I saw a golden blanket falling down on me and I had great peace. Then I heard another voice coming from inside me, probably the Holy Spirit, say, "This blanket is your prayer covering, the prayers of the people."

I did not know it, but my children had created a social media page about my health crisis to manage the deluge of questions and concern flooding in to them and the church. During the time of my vision, we were being overwhelmed by prayers and encouraging words online. That moment of torment by the enemy was the only anxiety I experienced.

Most anxiety comes from the voice of the enemy. The blanket of the prayers of my friends and well-wishers was comforting me, protecting me, and healing me, even in a medically controlled state as I hung between life and death. I exchanged my fear for the peace of His presence in my suffering. I exchanged my life for His life. I was at His mercy, life or death. And because of the prayers of His people, ministering angels, and the sweet Holy Spirit, I was at peace.

Isaiah saw the same One we will see if we are willing to grab on to Him for our very lives during times of difficulty and suffering. Isaiah saw Jesus! Jesus dried Isaiah's tears, changed his life, gave him knowledge by revelation, and showed him His love. When you walk through suffering along your journey together with God, the same blessings are yours. God's life will bring death to your flesh and then raise you up to walk out your new life with Him. His Word will come alive to you. He will make you an insider and show you the next step.

FINDING HIS PRESENCE DURING DISASTER

> For I know the thoughts that I think toward you, says the LORD, thoughts of peace and not of evil, to give you a future and a hope. Then you will call upon Me and go and pray to Me, and I will listen to you. And you will seek Me and find Me, when you search for Me with all your heart. I will be found by you, says the LORD, and I will bring you back from your captivity; I will gather you from all the nations and from all the places where I have driven you, says the LORD, and I will bring you

to the place from which I cause you to be carried away captive.

—JEREMIAH 29:11–14

The Bible is filled with examples of God's presence during disaster. The children of Israel discovered life wasn't easy, even for the chosen! They had lost their dream and had become a people captive to their enemy. In the middle of failure and disappointment, God spoke a word of hope: their dream from God was not destroyed, only delayed. Dealing with aftershocks of loss, failure, grief, and recovery can shake your faith and steal your dreams. Your God-given vision may have become distant and even imperceptible, and now you wonder whether your vision was ever meant to be. Grab hold of this word of hope and take steps to rediscover your dream! God still has plans for you—comfort comes if you can get into His presence and listen.

I will visit you and perform My good word toward you...

—JEREMIAH 29:10

Disaster doesn't define you. Everything He has said about you and promised you is still true! God's word will be fulfilled. His delays are not His denials. God will correct His children. But please remember, He will always keep His covenant with you! God is thinking good things about you! "'For I know the thoughts that I think toward you,' says the LORD, 'thoughts of peace and not of evil'" (Jer. 29:11). The God of this universe has you on His mind and heart! He longs for you to have the best in life. On your worst day when you feel like no one understands you, shares your dream, or has your best interests in mind, you can be assured that God is on your side! So climb up onto His lap and let His love comfort and reassure your heart.

Then embrace the gift of hope. His plan is "to give you a future and a hope" (v. 11). God's gift is a future filled with hope! Literally this translates to mean "an expected end." The Hebrew words for hope refer to a rope tied to "what is at the end." No matter what suffering you may experience in your life, your purpose is tied securely to God's eternal will! So, ask God for the help that you need, "then you will call upon Me and go and pray to Me, and I will listen to you" (v. 12). These words need no explanation! What an awesome promise to know God answers our prayers! Don't let the suffering drive you away from God. Seek God with all of your heart. "You will seek Me and find Me, when you search for Me with all your heart" (v. 13).

As you live out the principles above, you will begin to rediscover your dream and God's blessing in the suffering. Can you see that the future is not dimly lit but is bright with God's favor and guidance as you walk through with Him? Look beyond your struggle with confidence; God delights in you!

WAITING PRODUCES INTIMACY WITH GOD

Waiting is another season in life that can seem very painful and difficult, but it is in this season that we learn to trust the sovereignty of God. We learn God's character. This is the season when I am pressing God the most for attention, answers—anything! I am praying, seeking, in the Word, and keeping my ears peeled to the Spirit realm, desperate for any revelation God may have for me. This is how we get to know

God. Waiting creates an environment where we can position ourselves at the feet of our Father God.

Just this morning I was thinking about the first book I ever wrote and published. It was just after Paulette and I were married. That book on parenting was written before I had any children. After I had children of my own I hid all of the copies of that book that remained! Nothing like a little parenting practice to give you a new perspective! After that I wrote quite a number of other books, but it wasn't until almost thirty years after I wrote that first book that God really put His widespread blessing on what I was writing. The favor that I have now to reach a much larger readership has come through a lot of hard work, serving, and waiting. Has the content of my books changed? Yes and no. I still write from the Bible and life application, but the years of waiting, walking, and study have made the content richer and the revelation greater than it was with that first parenting book I wrote...before I was a parent!

Waiting is hard. We want success now. God gives us dreams and visions of what He is going to accomplish through our lives, and then we feel like He lets us down because what has been planted in our hearts doesn't manifest immediately. Well, I have good news for you today. You are not alone in the wait! Waiting should not discourage you from following after the Lord and believing in the dream. Life together with God will take you to some amazing places. You will have wonderful spiritual experiences. You will make a difference in the world around you. And then one day it will seem like you are simply on the shelf! We've already talked quite a bit about the apostle Paul, but let me take you back to him for an encouraging perspective on waiting.

WHAT PAUL'S LIFE CAN TEACH US ABOUT WAITING ON GOD

Paul spent three years in Arabia and a long period of time away from his homeland. It was over a decade before the church sent for him to begin the missionary journeys. What was going on during those ten years of silence? God was preparing Paul for something better! Paul was to carry the gospel to the population centers of the Western world.

He learned the lessons of life and ministry while waiting in the presence of Jesus. A man of letters and learning, he had to lay aside even the power of his intellect in order to learn Christ. He wrote to the church at Corinth humbly, in weakness and reverential fear, communicating that he had no wisdom of his own. His message and preaching weren't with wise or persuasive words. He came to demonstrate the power of the Holy Spirit, the only thing that could bring transformation. (See 1 Corinthians 2:12–16.)

Paul had experienced an intimate relationship with Jesus in the Holy Spirit. He had learned the things that cannot be discovered apart from that intimate life together with God. Paul spent over a decade alone with God so he could become a steward of God's mysteries (1 Cor. 4:1–2).

Paul could not talk in any detail about his intimate times with the Lord any more than we would talk about our intimacy with our mates! Yet Paul's letters resound with principles for living that sustain us today!

Heaven's power moves to earth when we wait with Jesus in that most holy place. Taking a walk through just one of Paul's letters, we discover powerful declarations of what he learned while he waited.

He learned to be thankful for his spiritual family.

> I thank my God every time I remember you. In all my prayers for all of you, I always pray with joy because of your partnership in the gospel from the first day until now, being confident of this, that he who began a good work in you will carry it on to completion until the day of Christ Jesus. It is right for me to feel this way about all of you, since I have you in my heart; for whether I am in chains or defending and confirming the gospel, all of you share in God's grace with me.
>
> —PHILIPPIANS 1:3–7, NIV

Too often we take our spiritual family for granted. Unfortunately, the twenty-first century church does not generally enjoy the kind of fellowship and loyalty that Paul is describing in this passage. I've said it many times, but I believe that many people view the church as nothing more than a social club—a place to be and be seen, rather than a place to serve, worship, and find genuine community.

He learned that prayer works!

> And this is my prayer: that your love may abound more and more in knowledge and depth of insight, so that you may be able to discern what is best and may be pure and blameless until the day of Christ, filled with the fruit of righteousness that comes through Jesus Christ—to the glory and praise of God....for I know that through your prayers and the help given by the Spirit of Jesus Christ, what has happened to me will turn out for my deliverance.
>
> —PHILIPPIANS 1:9–11, 19, NIV

There are not enough pages to express how personal this declaration is to me. I know for certain that I never would have made it this far in ministry without the deep, ongoing prayers of my family, church, and many people I will never know about until I reach heaven. I am so thankful that Jesus is at the right hand of the Father constantly praying for me.

He learned that trouble can lead to victory.

> Now I want you to know, brothers, that what has happened to me has really served to advance the gospel. As a result, it has become clear throughout the whole palace guard and to everyone else that I am in chains for Christ. Because of my chains, most of the brothers in the Lord have been encouraged to speak the word of God more courageously and fearlessly.
> —Philippians 1:12–14, niv

When we have a right response to the things that the enemy brings into our lives to limit our effectiveness, we will have a tremendous effect on the people around us. People are watching. Trust me! You can count on that situation where you want to lose your temper or set that person straight to be an opportunity for you to lose your testimony and destroy the reputation of your church. Think before you speak. This is a lesson I've learned the hard way a few times. You will gain a hearing with your enemies if you let the Holy Spirit control your words.

He learned not to fear death.

> I eagerly expect and hope that I will in no way be ashamed, but will have sufficient courage so that now as always Christ will be exalted in my body, whether by

life or by death. For to me, to live is Christ and to die
is gain.
—PHILIPPIANS 1:20–21, NIV

In recent days we have seen reports of Christians in the
Middle East being detained, beaten, threatened, and even
martyred simply for naming the name of Jesus. Christian
persecution is not something that is over. In fact, the Bible
warns us to expect these persecutions to come even more
frequently as the day of Christ's return approaches.

He learned that suffering is not always the result of sin.

For it has been granted to you on behalf of Christ not
only to believe on him, but also to suffer for him.
—PHILIPPIANS 1:29, NIV

Blaming the persecutions of life on a believer's uncon-
fessed sin is one of the most common mistakes we make in
the church world. The faith movement tells that if we just
have enough faith, everything will be OK. Sometimes faith
will remove our suffering. But the truth is, if we have enough
faith, God's Holy Spirit will also strengthen us to walk
through difficulty. Sometimes rain falls on the just. But the
just can live by faith.

He learned that he could think the thoughts of Jesus.

If you have any encouragement from being united with
Christ, if any comfort from his love, if any fellowship
with the Spirit, if any tenderness and compassion, then
make my joy complete by being like-minded, having the

same love, being one in spirit and purpose....Your attitude should be the same as that of Christ Jesus.

—Philippians 2:1–2, 5, NIV

Is your attitude always the same as that of Christ Jesus?
Well, this passage encourages us that it can be! It's a tall
order to strive for, but one that by grace we can move toward.
The Lord wants us to be likeminded, to have the same love
for one another and be in one spirit, united in our purpose
in the church.

He learned that God does the work in us.

It is God who works in you to will and to act according
to his good purpose.

—Philippians 2:13, NIV

This truth will set you free. Many Christ followers feel
defeated and inferior because we just aren't getting the work
done according to our time frame or plans! But that's where
we are getting sidestepped. It's not our plan, it's His that matters. And when we die to our plan, He is able to move us from
the shelf and use us in ways we would never have imagined.

**He learned that life at its best is knowing Christ
personally and intimately.**

But whatever was to my profit I now consider loss for
the sake of Christ. What is more, I consider everything
a loss compared to the surpassing greatness of knowing
Christ Jesus my Lord, for whose sake I have lost all
things. I consider them rubbish, that I may gain Christ
and be found in him, not having a righteousness of my
own that comes from the law, but that which is through

faith in Christ—the righteousness that comes from God
and is by faith. I want to know Christ and the power of
his resurrection and the fellowship of sharing in his sufferings, becoming like him in his death.
—PHILIPPIANS 3:7–10, NIV

My wife, Paulette, made Philippians 3:10 the theme of the
first women's conference that she hosted at our church: "I
want to know Christ and the power of his resurrection..."
Who doesn't want to know God more? But later she came
to understand that knowing God comes through diligence
and through becoming intimately acquainted with the sufferings of Jesus. We both have come to understand that the
sufferings we have experienced in our families and in ministry have brought us into a place of deeper spiritual intimacy
than we could have had if difficulty had not come. Neither of
us wanted bad things to happen. But those bad things have
resulted in growth, wisdom, and greater dependency on the
strong and loving power of God.

He learned not to quit!

Brothers, I do not consider myself yet to have taken
hold of it. But one thing I do: Forgetting what is behind
and straining toward what is ahead, I press on toward
the goal to win the prize for which God has called me
heavenward in Christ Jesus.
—PHILIPPIANS 3:13–14, NIV

Quitting is something that is rampant in our society.
Marriage gets tough—quit. Find another spouse. Work gets
hard—quit! Prayers don't get answered like I want—quit
praying. School demands too much of me—quit. Church

doesn't go like I want it to—quit going. And for many of us pastors, if pastoring the church leaves us feeling defeated and spiritually spent—quit...and go sell cars!

I've had that thought more than once across my long tenure here at Abba's House. I can't lie and tell you that every moment has been happy. We've always had a building project, and I feel like I've almost continuously carried the pressure of raising money. People who professed their loyalty have left me. Dear friends have experienced disease, loss, heartbreak, and death. And my filling with the Holy Spirit and personal awakening definitely proved that this passage is true.

Not everyone celebrated, understood, or embraced the Holy Spirit's work in my life and the subsequent work that followed in our church. Knowing God may cost you something. But what you gain is of so much greater and lasting value. The apostle Paul didn't, and I haven't yet—so don't quit!

He learned not to worry!

> Do not be anxious about anything, but in everything, by prayer and petition, with thanksgiving, present your requests to God. And the peace of God, which transcends all understanding, will guard your hearts and your minds in Christ Jesus.
> —PHILIPPIANS 4:6–7, NIV

If you have heard me preach either at Abba's House, through the streaming, or on our television broadcast, you have heard me talk honestly to you about worry. Faith is one of the greatest struggles I have experienced in recent years. It was a challenge for me not to worry about the financial condition of the church; my four-year-old grandson, Ryce, who had open heart surgery in 2012; and my own heart diagnosis and open heart surgery the same year.

Sometimes the enemy comes in with a flood of difficult circumstances and beats us over the head. Here in Philippians we are commanded, "Do not be anxious about anything..." That is pretty challenging and convicting.

As the senior pastor of the same church for over thirty years I would think I'd have this one down! But the truth is we all struggle at some point with letting go of the things that we cannot fix, change, or control. I want people to be "fixed" spiritually and in their circumstances. I want their hearts and minds to be "changed" by the love of Jesus. And as much as I'd like for every day to go without a wrinkle or conflict, I can't "control" that! What is the answer? Trust Jesus!

He learned to think right.

> Finally, brothers, whatever is true, whatever is noble, whatever is right, whatever is pure, whatever is lovely, whatever is admirable—if anything is excellent or praiseworthy—think about such things.
> —PHILIPPIANS 4:8, NIV

Paul understood that the battle is in the mind. Sin is not mindless activity. Every action is precipitated by a thought:

- Protect myself!
- No one will know!
- I deserve it!
- He or she deserves it!
- I don't care if it's wrong!

- It's my right!

- You can't make me!

Negative thoughts will result in negative actions and reactions. What are you thinking about?

- How bad life is, or what changes you can make to improve it?

- Who hurt you, or who blesses your life?

- What someone failed to do, or what God has done for you?

We must choose to think good thoughts.

He learned to be content.

> I am not saying this because I am in need, for I have learned to be content whatever the circumstances. I know what it is to be in need, and I know what it is to have plenty. I have learned the secret of being content in any and every situation, whether well fed or hungry, whether living in plenty or in want.
> —PHILIPPIANS 4:11–12, NIV

These were not just words that Paul had not lived out personally! He had suffered and enjoyed abundant prosperity and blessing. Even at the peril of his very life, Paul had found God to be enough. I believe that truth taken into our lives across time makes contentment possible.

Young children don't have any idea if their parents' bank account is full or empty. They just understand the love of mom and dad and the safety of their family. Even when there is shortage in a loving home, young children have an ability to adapt and be content in the circumstances.

In Philippians 4 Paul reveals the complex and varied experiences of his life and says, in effect, to the New Testament church and to us, "Your circumstances don't define you. Circumstances will always be changing. One day you will be on top of the world. The next you may find yourself in the pit of despair. But in both places you can have contentment if your faith is founded in the love of Jesus. You can trust in His plan for you.

He learned we could do anything Jesus asks us to do.

> I can do everything through him who gives me strength.
> —PHILIPPIANS 4:13, NIV

Do you see the progression here? Don't worry. Think right. Be content. Then, I can do anything Jesus asks me to! There are no limits with Him because I am learning that when He orders something, He pays for it. Know that sometimes other people aren't obedient to the will of God and impact what you are doing. But the joy is in the journey with Him. He will give you strength for every task. And that leads to the final thing that Paul tells us he had learned.

He learned that God is our source of supply.

> And my God will meet all your needs according to his glorious riches in Christ Jesus.
> —PHILIPPIANS 4:19, NIV

Paul learned all these fourteen great lessons of the abundant life as he walked a faithful and agreeable life with God.

These principles are ones you can live by as well. Remember, Paul wrote these thoughts down while in jail in Rome.

Your circumstances do not determine your attitude. You can worship and pray your way into the presence of God wherever you are! No matter the prison, the loneliness, or the turmoil you face in your life today, Jesus is waiting to meet you. Wait on Him to take the circumstances of your life and produce the beauty of His presence in your life. Waiting truly produces a life of agreement with God.

AGREEMENT WITH OTHERS

"Again I say to you that if two of you agree on earth concerning anything that they ask, it will be done for them by My Father in heaven. For where two or three are gathered together in My name, I am there in the midst of them."
—MATTHEW 18:19–20

S OME TIME AGO, Paulette and I were on a cruise ship going across the Atlantic. Every night they had shows. One night we went to a show put on by a concert pianist. He did a beautiful job—he played classics, sixties hits, and all kinds of music. Toward the end of the concert he said, "Now I want to play my favorite song for you." I was totally shocked when he began to play "Amazing Grace." But what was more amazing was what came after that.

Since we were sailing to England, a lot of people on board the ship were from Canada, Australia, or England. Most everyone in that eighteen-hundred-seat room started singing. In that moment the Lord spoke to me and said, "These people don't know each other, but this is the power of agreement." I could feel it. It was tangible. It was in the air. It didn't last long, but it was there.

Agreement isn't necessarily knowing everything about someone you agree with. Dr. Martin Luther King Jr.'s most famous speech is "I Have a Dream." He went to the grave with its message burning deep in his heart. He dreamed of seeing all races and ages of people find agreement around things that really matter in life.

If you look in the Bible, you will see that, from the first page of Genesis in the Creation account, agreement was God's highest value and attribute. The Hebrew word for God in this passage is *Elohim*, which is plural. God is God the Father, God the Son, and God the Holy Spirit—one in three and three in one. This models agreement.

The power of the Creator exists because there is a triune God who knows how to operate in His three persons in total harmony and agreement. So when He gets ready to make man, He doesn't say, "Let Me make man..." He says, "Let Us make man..." The creative power of God flowed out of Trinitarian agreement. Then if you read on, you'll see that it says, "God created man in His own image." We are body, soul, and spirit, but many of us live torn up all the time because we can't even agree with ourselves. After He said we would be made in His image, *then* it says, "Let *them* have dominion."

God gave us dominion, but we can't take dominion because we can't even agree on what a color a chair ought to be, much less take dominion of the earth. We can't keep our marriages together, and we're fussing about the Democrats and

Republicans. We have far more church splits in America than we have political splits.

Dominion comes and takeovers happen to nations when people put aside their personal stuff and get into agreement about what really matters.

Agreement is the most powerful word in the church world. The Greek word in Matthew 18:19 (the verse I used to open this section) is *sumphonia,* meaning "to say the same thing together." This is not about us all talking at the same time, but about us communicating the same thing in harmony— and we may not be communicating this in the same way.

If you think of members of a symphony doing their own thing and playing when they want to play, then you can imagine how confusing and unpleasant that sound would be. But when they all follow the conductor, they make a harmonious sound that is pleasing to the ear.

Being in agreement with others is about adjusting your life to operate in one accord with God and others. By nature we separate. We categorize one another. This is counterproductive to what God had in mind for the body of Christ. The devil knows this. He knows how to use agreement, if you don't. He uses two strategies to keep us out of unity with one another:

1. Procrastination. If he can get you to put something off, he will—not now, pay it later, do it later, tell them later, next Sunday...

2. Disagreement and disunity. God hates disagreement and disunity. We think He's upset about the gay agenda, R-rated movies, and the strip joint. No. You know what God hates? (See Proverbs 6:16–19.)

- A proud look
- A lying tongue
- Hands that shed innocent blood
- A heart that devises wicked plans (Do you ever get secretly happy when something bad happens to someone with whom you are not in agreement? That's a sin.)
- Feet that are swift in running to evil
- A false witness who speaks lies
- One who sows discord among brethren. Of everything in this list, this is the abomination. God hates those who sow discord

> Even so the tongue is a little member and boasts great things. See how great a forest a little fire kindles! And the tongue is a fire, a world of iniquity. The tongue is so set among our members that it defiles the whole body, and sets on fire the course of nature; and it is set on fire by hell.
>
> —JAMES 3:5–6

Division, gossip, slander—you have no right, no authority to say anything about anyone whom you haven't had the courage to go to personally. Disagreement makes us dwell in enmity with God.

We need the power of agreement in our lives. We need it in our marriages. If we don't get along with our wives, our prayers are hindered. We need to get into agreement in the body of Christ. We need to get our lives in harmony. We don't need to be looking at Washington until we get it right with ourselves first.

But it will take some work. This is what you need to understand about agreement:

1. Agreement requires death to self (Gal. 5:24).
   God is no respecter of persons. We are preju-
   diced people. We need to get over that idea of "I
   don't like her" or "I don't like him."

2. Agreement is a work of the Holy Spirit (Gal.
   5:25; Eph. 4). Unity was more important to Paul
   than denomination and doctrine. In Ephesians
   4:3 he said we should "endeavor to keep the
   unity of the Spirit in the bond of peace."

3. Agreement promotes success. (If any two of
   you get in symphony, I will do it. See Matthew
   18:19.) We'd rather be right than in symphony.
   We'd rather win the argument than get the
   release of God's power. We'd rather prove our
   point than have the anointing. We'd rather protect our turf like a bunch of animals marking
   our territory rather than let God be God in our
   lives.

4. Agreement brings God's presence (2 Cor. 13:11,
   14).

5. Agreement brings peace (Phil. 4:1–7). If you
   don't know anything about it, don't talk.

6. Agreement brings the commanded blessing.
   There are two things that bring a commanded
   blessing: (1) tithing 10 percent of your income.

(2) agreement and unity, the place of *sumphonia* (Ps. 133:1–3; see also Deut. 28; Lev. 25:21).

Bottom line is that we don't trust one another. What should we do about it? Die to it. "What if I get hurt again?" you may ask. It's worth the risk.

On the Day of Pentecost they were all in one accord, in harmony. What would happen if the people of God showed up and were ready to hear and do whatever God has for His church? We might just have an "and suddenly."

In this section we are going to learn what it takes to live in harmony with one another and the blessing that comes from it.

Chapter 9

AGREEMENT STARTS
IN YOUR HOME

By Ron Phillips and Ronnie Phillips Jr.

T HE SPIRITUAL AND social recovery of true family is necessary for the survival of our culture. It is not surprising that Satan's first attack was dividing husband and wife, and his infernal strategy remains the same.

The principle of being in agreement with God and others must be lived out first in the home! There is a biblical pattern for relationship in the family, and there is a promised blessing and special favor on families that embrace these truths.

Just as God has a design for our life with Him and with others, He also has a design for our life as a family. Our success with our families is very much linked to our relationship with God and the church. A house does not make a home, just as a wedding ceremony does not guarantee a happy marriage. A faithful, fulfilled, and fruitful family is possible only if there can be a return to the manual written by the One who instituted the family from the beginning. The Bible is God's manual for families.

The psalmist said, "Unless the LORD builds the house, they labor in vain who build it" (Ps. 127:1).

In the Bible the family was a corporate unit that served as the center of social and religious training. The laws of the Old Testament sought to preserve and strengthen the family ties. In the New Testament, Jesus gave advice for the home in His teaching. He rebuked men for their practice of divorce. He raised the level of womanhood by both word and deed. He exercised the compassion of a father upon the little children He encountered. He loved His own mother dearly, and He wanted to make sure she was taken care of, even as He was facing death Himself.

Twentieth century conditions are different than those of the Old Testament and New Testament to some degree. The population explosion and cultural demands have made the biblical ideal of a large family difficult. The shift from an agricultural setting to an urban, industrialized setting has now made the large family an economic concern. Increased transportation has relocated and spread the family to the extent that multigenerational families are less often living close to one another. The family is now a smaller unit with fewer ties to tradition. Most families now have two parents who work outside the home, so there is more shared responsibility in earning a living as well as maintaining the home.

These trends have brought some challenges to the family. There is more of a struggle for unity and solidarity, as families are pulled so many different directions. The lack of expression of parental authority has undermined traditional relationships. Children are given over to day care and educational institutions for rearing. The husband becomes a slave to his work in order to meet the ever-burgeoning needs of his family. The mother often feels guilty for not spending more time with her children. Unfortunately, this often results in divorce, suicide, juvenile crime, and lonely despair.

The Bible sets forth some tools that can help build and strengthen families in the midst of such circumstances. God has given us in Scripture the guidelines and structure for a solid foundation in marriage and family. Love is the glue that binds the family together, as there is both authority and tenderness. Being part of a family is both a privilege and a responsibility. It is God's plan for our lives, and it is meant to be enjoyable and fulfilling.

Having a loving, cohesive marriage is the foundation of a happy family.

DEVELOPING YOUR MARRIAGE

God designed marriage to be celebrated and enjoyed. We see in Genesis 2:18–25 that it was the first institution God created on earth. Then in the New Testament in Ephesians 5:22–33, Paul gave instructions for marriage. He confirmed that the husband was the authority in the home (Eph. 5:23; Col. 3:18). This was qualified by additional statements affirming the husband to be under the lordship of Christ and directing the husband to love the wife with the same kind of love as Christ had for the church (Eph. 5:23–25). However, this authority did not extend to the spiritual realm, for "there is neither male nor female; for you are all one in Christ Jesus" (Gal. 3:28). Equality was also affirmed in relation to the marriage bed (1 Cor. 7:1–5). Authority over the children was also equal. Children were to obey the commands of their parents without question, without exception, and without complaint (Eph. 6:1; Col. 3:20). Parents were to love, discipline, and instruct their children in the ways of the Lord (Eph. 6:4).

This is the ideal God has set forth for both husband and wife. With His help, we should strive for that ideal.

Love your wife as Christ loved the church.

The husband is commanded to love his wife as Christ loved the church. This is the greatest demand upon the man. The love of Christ demonstrates for a man the nature of his love for his family. So what does this love look like when applied to a husband?

The love of Christ is sacrificial. Christ died for the church. He laid down His life for her life. Thus, every man should be willing to lay his life down for his wife and family. He gives his life in labor to provide for his family. A man should sacrifice himself for his family. So many sacrifice themselves for a job or a hobby, yet our lives belong to our families.

The love of Christ is faithful. Christ doesn't quit loving us because we fail or disappoint Him. He goes on loving us into His likeness. Many are unfaithful to their wives today; they claim that they fall out of love. The truth is that they don't know what real love is. Genuine love is faithful in the face of great difficulties.

The love of Christ is transforming. Christ's love for the church is cleansing her, removing every spot and wrinkle. So a man's faithful and sacrificial love will make his wife a better and more beautiful person. A woman who is greatly loved will radiate a beauty and glow that no cosmetic could ever give.

Most emotional problems wives have could be solved if

they could be secure in their husband's love. If they know that their husband loves them, they can face life's obstacles. A woman needs to be told and shown that she is loved. Most women today feel used rather than loved. It is like the boy who was looking at a photo album with his dad. He saw a picture of his dad and mother shortly after they were married and he asked, "Dad, is that when Mother came to work for us?" The wife should know that she is loved. It should be evident not only in words, but in deed.

When a man loves a woman, he will be her provider in four key areas. (See Ephesians 5:29–33.)

1. Physical provision (v. 29). A man is called on to nourish his wife and family. The word nourish means to rear and feed. The husband is to see that his family is provided with shelter, clothing, and food.

2. Emotional provision (v. 29). The man is instructed to cherish his family. *Cherish* means to spread wings over, as a bird does the nest. The husband is to protect his family. The family should feel secure and safe. A man should express appreciation and consideration toward his wife and meet her emotional needs, as well as the needs of his children.

3. Sexual provision (1 Pet. 3:7). The verse in 1 Peter 3:7 is a veiled reference to sexual relations. A man ought to know how to love his wife physically. She should feel like a queen with him. She

should know that he greatly desires her. A man's
wife should be his greatest earthly treasure.

4. Spiritual provision. The husband is to be the
   spiritual leader of his home. It is every man's
   job to meet his family's spiritual needs. A family
   is sustained by the example of a Spirit-filled
   father. Furthermore, his prayers and his reading
   of God's Word should be a daily practice, for his
   own benefit as well as the leadership example he
   is to set for his wife and children. It is his job to
   build his family up through God's teaching and
   promises. When a man leads as he is called, his
   wife will want to follow and respect him.

Be the wife God desires you to be.

Solomon asked the question long ago, "Who can find a vir-
tuous woman?" (Prov. 31:10–31). He then stated that a woman
of character is priceless. The most valuable stone in the
Middle East was the Oriental ruby, and Solomon estimated
the value of this special woman to be more than "rubies." The
search today would be even more difficult.

These days, women face many struggles: identity, modesty,
responsibility, and not living under the authority and protection of their husband. The answer to these struggles is for a
woman to be what God desires her to be and thus find ful-
fillment. Looking at Solomon's account in Proverbs 31 of the
happy woman, we can see some hope for a fulfilled life.

When she loves as God has called her to, a wife will find
that her husband depends on her. He trusts her. "The heart
of her husband safely trusts her; so he will have no lack of
gain. She does him good and not evil all the days of her life"

(v. 11–12). According to verse 23, he is very proud of her. She is the cause of great honor to him. When he passes through the city, the other men remark how fortunate he is to have found such a wife. She is so wonderful that her praise is constantly on his lips. He tells her that she is the best woman in the world.

Over and over the hands of this remarkable woman are mentioned. They are busy hands, for she works hard. See Proverbs 31:13, 16, and 20. Indeed, they are beautiful hands. They are protective and purposeful hands.

How very important are the hands of a wife and mother. Her touch and caress brush the tears from the eyes of her children. She helps bring peace to the worried brow of a weary husband. The woman of character is never indolent, but useful. She is proud of being a woman and the governess of her family. She is not a slave, but a queen.

The ideal wife not only takes care of others but also takes care of herself (v. 22). She keeps herself attractive for herself and for her husband. She has a joyful and optimistic outlook (vv. 25–26). She says the right things at the right time. The admirable wife has no time for gossip. Her children bless her (v. 28).

The secret of this woman's life is her "fear" or reverence for the Lord (v. 30). She is a godly woman. No woman can be complete until she bows at the feet of the Lord Jesus Christ. He is the champion of true freedom. This freedom is not a freedom from responsibility, but a freedom *for* responsibility. This is not a negative freedom, "not to be," but a freedom "to be" woman. It is a liberty that releases the woman to be more through Him.

God designed men and women differently, with specific

purposes in mind. He has given us clear instructions as to our roles as husbands and wives. We must take this information and constantly review it, putting ourselves to the test to see if we are living up to all God called us to be. We must also ensure we are growing in our own spiritual journey. We must attend to our own spiritual needs so we can be nourished in our spirit and adequately attend to the needs of our spouse and children.

THREE PRINCIPLES FOR BUILDING A STRONG FAMILY

The first is the principle of authority. The home must be regulated according to Scripture. Christ must be at the center of the home as Lord. The husband is to be the head of his family. The wife is to be submissive to her husband. The children are to be obedient to their parents. Anything with two heads is a monster! I am convinced when God's order of authority is established in the home, revival will come. Dr. Emerson Eggerichs calls a lack of love and respect in a home the Crazy Cycle. Without love, she reacts; without respect, he reacts; and the cycle goes on and on until it is broken.[1]

The principle of affection is next. A home must have warmth and love. Authority and discipline must be administered in such a way that warmth and love are demonstrated. The primary need of a woman is affection. The husband should give his wife the attention that lets her know he cares. A husband should never be as rude as the old farmer who hurt his wife's feelings. As they walked along one day she said, "Honey, we've been married forty years, why don't we kill the hog?" Of course, she meant to celebrate the anniversary, but the rough old man answered, "It's bad, but I don't see why we ought to kill the poor old hog over it." Husband and wife should be affectionate to each other and to their children. There ought to be love, hugs, laughter, and kisses.

Third is the principle of admonition. To admonish means to caution, to counsel, to rebuke with mildness, and to inform by warning. The home is to be a place where the family is admonished from the Word of God. Our families must not simply be told not to do something, but should be shown from the Scripture the consequences of evil.

PROTECTING YOUR FAMILY

At the dawn of creation God established the family as the earth's first social institution. Before sin hurled its death-dealing spear into the heart of humanity, the family was established by the hand of God. Therefore, it should be no surprise that the archfiend of hell chose the family as the canvas on which to paint his black and bloody designs.

The twentieth century witnessed the deterioration and dissolution of the family. Now, in the twenty-first century, the divorce rate in America remains around 50 percent. The average house in America does not contain a home or a family. It is filled with heated argument, icy silence, rebellion, insolence, and unhappiness. The family's god is pleasure, its goal is money and possessions, and its altar is the television. The average child in America watches fifteen hundred hours of television a year, yet only has a meaningful conversation with a parent 3.5 minutes a week![2] No wonder our nation is on such a moral landslide. The Bible has been displaced by the magazine, prayer by the telephone, and faith by the credit card. Church is attended only if it is convenient. The homes of many are little oceans with each member a little island of selfishness. Christ is unwelcome and unknown.

In my hometown, a lovely old home was being torn down. I stopped by to see it before the demolition crew did their work. It had a fresh coat of paint and seemed to be in good shape. Some workers were there salvaging some of the decorative trim. I asked them why this old home had to be torn down. They replied, "It was a well-constructed old home, but termites and moisture have rotted the floor and framing of this place." They showed me a wall that had been removed, revealing all of the decaying wood in that wall. I walked outside and looked at the beautiful white old structure glistening in the sunshine and thought, "One would never know that this old place was rotten and about to collapse."

Later as I drove along I thought, "How many homes are like that old house, with an outward veneer of respectability and inside rotten with problems?" The modern home has "termites" that eat away at the foundations of the family. Many families have an appearance of stability, but inside is turmoil and hostility. Churches and communities all over America are shocked to see the veneer of respectability ripped away from their leading families by the strong hand of marital discord.

Satan has unleashed the power and resources of hell on the family. Broken homes are becoming more common among professing Christians. Satan knows that a disruption of the home yields three infernal results:

1. First, the Word of God is blasphemed (Titus 2:5, KJV). "To be discreet, chaste, keepers at home,

good, obedient to their own husbands, that the
word of God be not blasphemed."

2. Second, prayers are hindered (1 Pet. 3:7, KJV).
"Likewise, ye husbands, dwell with them
according to knowledge, giving honour unto the
wife, as unto the weaker vessel, and as being
heirs together of the grace of life; that your
prayers be not hindered."

3. Third, the next generation is robbed of a good
and long life (Eph. 6:1–3). "Children, obey your
parents in the Lord, for this is right. 'Honor
your father and mother,' which is the first com-
mandment with promise: 'that it may be well
with you and you may live long on the earth.'"

How Satan laughs at and mocks those trying to live the
Christian life with things not right at home.

A recent study revealed the causes for divorce. The three
major causes, in layman's terms rather than legal terms, are
alcohol, finances, and sexual problems. These causes are dis-
guised under many high-sounding phrases such as incompatibility of temperament, mental cruelty, and alienation of
affection. Incompatibility of temperament is a nice way of
saying the other party is a drunkard. Mental cruelty means a
lot of things, but it can mean that one of the parties is stingy.
Alienation of affections is a polite term for adultery.

These, however, are not root causes of broken homes. The
root cause of a broken home is selfishness—people insistent
upon living for their own benefit and desires.

Love: A Family's Most Powerful Weapon Against Disunity

The state of our families is desperate but not hopeless. The house can become a home. Man, woman, and child can become a family.

John 3:16 states, "God so loved the world that He gave." God gave His best, His Son, as a lavish display of love. John 3:16 says that we perceive and understand love when we see the sacrifice of Jesus Christ. The opposite of selfishness is love. God's kind of love is self-giving and self-sacrificing. We practice that love when we are willing to "lay our lives down" for others.

The only way selfishness can be slain is for the love of God to be poured into a heart. Romans 5:5 states, "Now hope does not disappoint, because the love of God has been poured out in our hearts by the Holy Spirit who was given to us."

Every born-again person has the capacity to love self-sacrificially. When the love of God is present in the heart and home, we have access to formidable weapons with which to combat the enemies of the home. The home's enemy is selfishness, the only weapon is love, and the only way we can have that love is through Jesus Christ.

To ensure the enemy doesn't make headway in your marriage and your family, you must remain proactive in removing stumbling blocks and potential temptations or distractions. Your marriage and your family are gifts worthy of protecting. They deserve your best effort and attention. God designed marriage, and He led you to one another. He is on your side, and this is a love worth fighting for.

How to Restore Family Relationships

Since marriage is the center of most families, I will use marriage as the example of how to restore unity and agreement between family members. The principles are universal. For this, I will refer to Song of Solomon 6–7.

1. The parties in conflict must surrender their rights to each other (Song of Sol. 6:1–3). In verse 3, Shulamith stresses mutual possession when she says that she belongs to him, and he belongs to her. This is the same principle that Paul used in 1 Corinthians 7:4 when he said that the wife has authority over the husband's body and the husband has authority over the wife's body.

2. Both parties must have a forgiving attitude (Song of Sol. 6:4–9). Solomon receives her without rebuking her, and immediately he restores communication with sweet compliments. Understanding is necessary if broken relationships are to be mended. Notice his request for her not to look at him (v. 5). Her look fills him with desire, and he does not want a physical relationship until fellowship has been restored.

3. Both parties must regain oneness in spirit (Song of Sol. 6:10–13). In this section, Shulamith is seen in Solomon's chariot. They are back together. Note in verse 13 that she is called "Shulamith." That is the feminine form of the

name Solomon. This is a beautiful allusion
to the fact that they were one flesh as God
intended.

Once these other steps of restoration have been taken, then
there can be growth toward intimacy and affection. When
family members can restore their relationships rather than
run from conflict and hurt, that is when there is maturity.

The Bible instructs us that all bitterness, anger, malice,
and ill feelings must be put under the blood of Christ. (See
Ephesians 4:31.) Offended parties should be confronted and
forgiveness asked. Until the steps to a clear conscience and
a cleansed heart are taken, the person cannot have true joy.
Life can take on a new thrill and a new exhilaration. Real
life can be discovered. This real life is found only in commit-
ments to Jesus Christ and recommitments to one another.

When someone breaks a bone, physicians say that the
bone is even stronger once it heals. The area that recon-
nects is made stronger by the way the calcium wraps it and
strengthens it. So can a relationship that was broken then
heal and be stronger than it ever was before. As you recon-
nect, God can wrap you in His love. "A threefold cord is not
quickly broken" (Eccles. 4:12).

I know of a home that is broken today in another city. One
child is in jail, another is mentally disturbed, and another
will have nothing to do with either parent. The husband was
unfaithful. Later, he was saved. God forgave him, but his wife
was unable to forgive him. Eventually her attitude divided
her home and destroyed their children.

No family can survive that does not practice forgiveness daily. Ephesians 4:31–32 is a passage that should be

memorized by each family member: "Let all bitterness, and wrath, and anger, and clamor, and evil speaking, be put away from you, with all malice: And be ye kind one to another, tenderhearted, forgiving one another, even as God for Christ's sake hath forgiven you" (KJV).

Love carries on by word and example to the next generation of family. It *never* fails. You never make the wrong choice when you choose to act in love. Love God. Love the church. Love your spouse and kids. Leave a legacy—one that will not fail!

TEACHING AGREEMENT TO THE NEXT GENERATION

Psalm 127:3 states, "Behold, children are a heritage from the LORD, the fruit of the womb is a reward."

Children were status symbols in the Old Testament (Ps. 127:3–5). Sons were most highly regarded, because the firstborn son was the one through whom the lineage of the family was to be continued. Children were expected to love, respect, and obey their parents, and there were penalties for disobedience.

> Children, obey your parents in the Lord; for this is right. "Honor your father and mother," which is the first commandment with promise: "that it may be well with you and you may live long on the earth." And you, fathers, do not provoke your children to wrath, but bring them up in the training and admonition of the Lord.
> —EPHESIANS 6:1–4

It is the first duty of children to obey their parents. Paul declares that this is the right thing to do. Obedience to parents is one of the Ten Commandments (Exod. 20:12). It is God's desire that every child be obedient to his parents. "My son, hear the instruction of your father, and do not forsake the law of your mother" (Prov. 1:8). This obedience is to be absolute. Colossians 3:18 states that children are to be obedient "in all things."

It is a grievous thing for a child to despise the authority of his parents. God compares a person's joy in life and length of life with obedience. Ephesians 6:3 states, "That it may be well with you." A child who lives a stubborn and rebellious life cannot be at peace with himself or God. Life will not seem good to him until there is obedience.

The second duty of children is to honor their parents. The verb *honor* means "to value." It means to heap worth and value on someone. It is used to describe how a Christian ought to treat Christ.

A child demonstrates honor for his parents in two ways. The first is by respecting their authority. God pronounced the death sentence on children who did not respect their parents. Leviticus 20:9 says: "For everyone who curses his father or his mother shall be surely put to death. He has cursed his father or mother. His blood shall be upon him."

A child also demonstrates honor by showing appreciation. Parents receive honor when their children appreciate their sacrifices. Proverbs 19:26 warns against "wasting father and chasing way mother." This is a spirit of ungratefulness.

Parents must aid their children in doing their duties within the family unit. This is accomplished through love and discipline. Love and discipline work together to bring the child to maturity. This discipline will put protective boundaries around your children. It makes them secure and content.

Obedience, honor, and respect are forms of submission to authority and a gateway to being able to submit laterally to those with whom you interact on a regular basis. If we could get this down as children, imagine how much easier it would be for us as we work and serve within the body of Christ. This is a key to being able to walk in agreement with others.

A Godly Home Is a Reflection of the Plan of Salvation

When a home has a saved father who is sacrificing and loving his family as Jesus loved the church and a saved mother submissively serving and loving her husband, then the children see a pattern of salvation. There is no more powerful presentation of the gospel than a Christ-centered home.

Let the family live the gospel of Jesus Christ. Let His presence be the source of family joy. Let His forgiveness not only be received but also passed on to the sinful and erring. Let His peace and unity be the secret of contentment and satisfaction. Let His Word be lovingly received, gratefully shared, and completely obeyed. May every home erect an altar to Him and daily meet Him in prayer. Let the home become a lighthouse to the lost and a living testimony to the power of God through unity and agreement.

Children are a blessing from the Lord, and they give us a little bit of insight into how God must love us. "If you then, who are evil, know how to give good gifts to your children, how much more will the heavenly Father give the Holy Spirit to those who ask Him!" (Luke 11:13, RSV). As parents, we know there is nothing our kids could do to make us cease loving them. Romans 8:39 says, "Neither height nor depth, nor anything else in all creation, will be able to separate us from the love of God that is in Christ Jesus our Lord" (NIV).

Let's be thankful for the gift of family and what it can teach us about the power of agreement. If we can't get it right in our homes first, we will not get it right in the body of Christ as a whole. Let's be good examples to our kids so they will learn from us and pass it on to the next generation of believers.

Chapter 10

BEYOND YOU AND YOURS

By Ronnie Phillips Jr.

NTIMACY WITH GOD will often lead to intimacy with others. There are times when the Lord will send you strength or encouragement through a friend with "skin on." One of the most valuable resources in life is the strength found in quality relationships with others. These special people God sends us during difficult times are called soul mates. In the darkest moments of my life, Jesus showed up in the form of a soul mate. These kinds of relationships breed a level of agreement in your life that is not easily duplicated. These are the kinds of connections we should value, cultivate, nurture, and protect.

It was 1997 leading into my junior year of high school. I had been named the starting center for a nationally and state-ranked high school football team. I wasn't very big, but I loved the game of football and my teammates. I also respected and loved our head coach, who had transformed our losing high school football program into a winning program. He had a way of building you up after he tore you down. He believed in me, and although I was very small compared to the other linemen, he knew I had what it takes to be a football player: heart, motivation, and leadership.

There's something to be said about teachers and coaches who by example push us toward our dreams and aspirations. Perhaps John Quincy Adams, our nation's sixth president, said it best concerning leadership: "If your actions inspire others to dream more, learn more, do more, and become more, you are a leader."[1] My coach was a leader, and he was able to identify and promote those characteristics in me. He motivated me to achieve things I would have never achieved without his help. It is impossible to measure the influence he had on my life.

Winning may not be everything, but it matters, and we won a lot of football games. Our team was ranked higher than it had ever been ranked before. Things were going great for me personally, and I was looking forward to finishing my high school football career and playing football at a small college.

One night while driving to get some food with some friends, I began to speed through a neighborhood, and I flipped my Isuzu Trooper down a fifteen-foot embankment. The accident was very scary, and I was lucky to have lived. I severed my wrist, fractured my knee, and tore some ligaments. I was not drinking alcohol or anything of that nature, but rumors spread throughout the church. I was a preacher's kid in a small town, so I had become very aware of how hateful church folks could be and how quickly lies could spread.

The next morning, the head coach who had inspired me resigned and moved out of the state. He called and checked on me and encouraged me, but I was devastated that he was leaving. Suddenly it seemed like everything was caving in around me, and I was most certainly under an attack from the enemy. Things may seem much bigger than they are during our teenage years, but what I was feeling at that moment was very real. I was devastated for two reasons: (1) because of how close my previous coach and I were, and (2) because the new head coach was a former assistant coach who hated my father's ministry and me. The inescapable fact that my father was the local pastor of one of the largest churches in the state of Tennessee is a blessing, but it has also been a challenge as those who have been against God's work have so often been draconian in their remarks and their treatment of my family and me. Football had been a healthy activity to escape the pressure of being a preacher's kid, and the football field was a great place to release stress. Now football was a source of constant harassment and sarcasm.

This new coach would often make fun of my family during practices, and he made jokes about the ministry. I knew that I would never get a fair shake with this man. He didn't care for me, and I didn't care for him. In my opinion, this man was completely unproven as a coach. Over the next two years more than half of the players would quit. This man eventually left coaching well after I graduated, but the effects of the five years he was at this high school can still be felt today. My high school football team did not win a championship during his tenure, and since his departure the program has cycled through five coaches. It took years for the team to recover.

John J. Pershing, the only person to ever be promoted in his lifetime to the highest rank in the United States Army (General of the Armies) once said, "A competent leader can get efficient service from poor troops, while on the contrary an incapable leader can demoralize the best of troops."[2] I was demoralized to say the least. Nothing positive can come from negative leadership.

The car accident and the news of my coach leaving happened within forty-eight hours of each other, and even though I was lucky to be alive, I was extremely depressed, and I felt like my life was over. Thankfully, when I was at my lowest moment, a knock came to my door. It was five of my best friends who came into my home and encouraged me, made jokes, and lifted my spirit.

Through this experience, I learned that there are soul mates or friends who will come and lift you up during the most difficult times of your life, but that there are also people whom the enemy uses to curse you and keep you from becoming all that God wants you to be. Poet and playwright William Shakespeare said this about friendship: "Words are easy, like the wind; faithful friends are hard to find."[3] In this chapter, I want to give you four basic elements of friendship, as well as discuss the qualities of God's friendship to us.

1. Enjoying the Company of Another

Many of us have people with whom we enjoy doing things such as shopping, golfing, fishing, hunting, nails, hair, etc. All of us have people with whom we enjoy doing certain things. Many people who frequent bars have what are called drinking buddies, and these are men or women who like to "party" and have that interest in common with other people. Sometimes misery loves company. Just because you have activities in common doesn't mean you are real friends and can walk in the power of godly agreement.

If you absolutely have to be doing something to enjoy the company of another, it may be the activity that attracts you, not the personality. If you don't enjoy the company of someone then you need to keep a safe distance between him and you. If God sends you someone, then you will know it and there will be an inner joy that you feel when that person is around that has nothing to do with the activity in which you are engaged.

2. Lifting Up Another

Another characteristic of true friendship is the betterment of the other. Quality connections improve both people involved. One of the most devastating actions that hinders personal development is being in relationship with the wrong people.

One of the most difficult things I struggle with as a pastor is living in the town in which I was raised and the *tie* to friends from my past. Many of my friends have come to know the Lord and they are serving Him in the ministry, but some just use me and take advantage of my gift of mercy.

Solid friendships lead to mutual improvement. You should be able to say to a friend, "I am better because of you." Likewise your friend should be better because of you. Proverbs 27:17 reflects this concept as well: "As iron sharpens iron, so one man sharpens another" (NIV). Are you being challenged by the people in your life? Are they building you up, or tearing you down? A genuine friendship is about building each other up, not tearing each other down. J. Willard Marriot, American entrepreneur and businessman who founded Marriot International, said, "Choose your friends wisely. They'll make or break you."[4] Real relationships produce life-changing results.

3. Sharing a Unified Purpose and Destiny

Lasting friendships are marked by a sense of destiny. The mystery of friendship is rooted in divine providence, which could be defined as God bringing people together by His Spirit and unifying them for a purpose that is much larger than anything they could have ever done on their own. It is the favor that very few people get to experience. This is the ability to share in God's plan and His destiny.

Perhaps the greatest example of friendship in the Old Testament was David and Jonathan in 1 Samuel 18:1–2. David's and Jonathan's lives were bound together in destiny. They had a shared sense of destiny that we will discuss in a later chapter. God brings certain people across your path with whom you will share a lifetime connection.

Sharing a common faith, a common destiny, and common goals with others will enrich your life and lead you toward your destiny. It's easy to become selfish and ask questions such as, "Who is helping me achieve my destiny?" But I find it best to begin with this question: "Whom am I helping achieve their destiny?"

I wasn't just working for myself when I played on my high school football team. I was helping my teammates, the school, and yes, that wonderful coach who was pouring so much into my life. We played football with a sense of destiny. Through typical athletic ups and downs, we were in it together. Congressman and former vice-presidential candidate Paul Ryan said, "Every successful individual knows that his or her achievement depends on a community of persons working together."[5]

4. BEING THERE IN THE TRENCHES

Some of my friends from high school and church who serve or have served in the military tell me that there is an uncommon bond between soldiers, sailors, and marines who have "endured the fight." An example of this is a book written by Stephen Ambrose and a miniseries of the same name produced by Steven Spielberg and Tom Hanks called *Band of Brothers.*

The book and miniseries follow the 506th Parachute Regiment of the 101st Airborne Division during the invasion of Normandy and the eventual destruction of Nazi Germany. *Band of Brothers* doesn't just focus on the selflessness of soldiers who often paid the ultimate price for our freedom, but it also displays the heroics of men surrendering their lives for one another.

Decades later and on a different battlefield Lieutenant Colonel Hal Moore, commander of the 1st Battalion, 7th Cavalry Regiment, at the Battle of Ia Drang in Vietnam, said this about soldiers: "American soldiers don't fight for what some president says on TV, they don't fight for mom, apple pie, or the American flag...they fight for one another."[6] Soldiers, sailors, and marines have a shared sense of destiny.

As Christians, we too are in a battle, though it is not one of flesh and blood (Eph. 6:12). These battles are not waged against us by coincidence. Often they are planned, coordinated attacks by the enemy to prevent us from achieving our destiny. Whom we stand with in the trenches helps to determine the outcome of the battle and helps to shape our destiny.

God has placed people all around us who have great potential in Christ. So often we are so consumed with our own ambitions that we fail to see others who are also pursuing God's purpose or destiny. These are the men and women who are in the spiritual trenches beside us, behind us, or in front of us. Yes, we need their help, but they need our help as well.

Whom are you assisting in the trenches? Whom are you willing to assist with prayer, time, and treasure? Are you fighting for your own personal gain, or are you in the trenches for the spiritual soldiers beside you or the leaders in front of you? Have you left anyone behind on the field of battle?

The battle is won when we fight for one another, sharing a common goal or destiny.

Accomplishing great things, pursuing unimaginable dreams, and reaching unobtainable goals begins with helping others do the same. Zig Ziglar, American author and motivational speaker, once said, "If you go looking for a friend, you're going to find they're scarce. If you go out to be a friend, you'll find them everywhere."[7] One of the easiest ways to find genuine friendships is to be a genuine friend.

Here are some questions you must ask yourself about the people in your life:

1. Do they enjoy your company or what you can do for them?

2. Do they get offended with you when you don't agree with them? The friend who gets offended is usually the last one to forgive.

3. Do they celebrate you or tolerate you? Go where you are celebrated, not tolerated.

4. Do they talk bad about other people to you? If people talk about others to you, then they are talking about you to others. That is a trust issue.

5. Do they congratulate you when God blesses you? If they aren't happy for your success, then they will rejoice when you fail.

6. Do they contribute anything (support, encouragement, prayer, love, service, financial aid, or general assistance in your day-to-day activities) to your life? If you are the one doing for them and they never reciprocate, you are in a codependent relationship. A codependent relationship is a relationship in which one is emotionally dependent on another person.

7. Do they love and are they serving God and advancing His kingdom? Notice that I didn't ask if they believed. In our Western culture, "belief" is cheap. Are they serving God and growing closer to Him every day? If not, keep a safe distance, never forgetting Ephesians 5:11: "And have no fellowship with the unfruitful works of darkness, but rather reprove them" (KJV). The New Testament states this truth simply: "Bad company corrupts good character" (1 Cor. 15:33, NIV). A friend who is a winner will make you a winner. A friend who is a loser will make you a loser.

Pursuing godly friends who challenge you or who want you to be more than you ever imagined is a difficult task, and it may mean that you will lose some people in your life who are not being the godly friends you need. Remember that there are certain friends for certain seasons in our life. In this case, be thankful for your time together, but do not be afraid to move on. At times, this is a painful process. But don't let nostalgia dictate your relationships. Just because you shared a locker twenty years ago doesn't mean you're on the same biblical path as the other person. Furthermore, just because you went to Bible school with someone doesn't mean you share the same vision for what God wants to do with your life.

Being a godly friend is also a great task and it requires a great sacrifice, but it's worth it in those dreadful moments of frustration and terror that grip us on the road toward our destiny. Have friends who want to be challenged and aren't afraid to receive biblical instruction and correction, but also be the friend who wants to be challenged and will listen.

Levels of Friendships

The following list of the basic levels of friendship did not originate from me but are found in many works on relationships. I first heard these from the noted teacher Bill Gothard at his Institute in Basic Life Principles conference. This list can help you determine the rightful place for the different people in your life:

Acquaintance

This category includes those individuals you know at the simplest level, and all friendships begin here. You recognize them and they recognize you. You may know scores of people this way. Acquaintances are important and significant. Without even knowing it, you may influence these

people in life-changing ways. Consider that coworker you
see every other day by the soda machine, or the mother who
drops her child off at the day care the same time as you do,
or the student who sits two rows ahead of you in economics
class. These individuals are watching you, and they know
more about what you live and believe than you may imagine.
Remember, you may be the only Jesus that these people ever
see.

Casual

These friends you see more often, but your relationship is
still on the surface. These friends have more contact with
you. At work, school, and church, most of our friendships are
casual. We know the casual friend by name, and usually we
know some facts about his life, yet there is not openness with
that person. You may share a hobby or activity together such
as golf, but you have little knowledge about his background
or family.

Close

A close friend should be one with whom you share common
values and goals. At this stage, the circle gets smaller. This
core group includes those who share a commitment to the
same basic philosophy and moral standards. Normally this
person is either a believer in Christ or sympathetic to the
message of Jesus. You feel this person is going in the same
direction as you are. You enjoy being around close friends
because they encourage you and you encourage them.

Intimate

An intimate friend is someone with whom you can share
your heart and soul. The term used today is *soul mates.*

Aristotle said that intimate friends are "a single soul dwelling in two bodies."[8] Marital partners ought to be at this level of friendship before they marry. Sexual relationships should always come after marriage. Too many couples confuse sex with intimacy. It is possible to be attracted to a person, marry that person, and have sex with that person, and yet not be intimate friends! This is the reason so many marriages break up or are unhappy. The unhappy couple may be sex mates but not soul mates. It is imperative that engaged couples become intimate friends before they make the marital commitment and sexual union. Intimate friends should reach beyond one's family ties. All of us need a few people with whom we can be transparent.

Sharers of destiny

I add this deeper level of friendship beyond the intimate level. I believe in the mystery of friendship. There are some people who come along to be your partner in the destiny to which God has called you. These are friends for life. These are special people with whom you can share your heart and soul as well as laugh, weep, *be* stupid, and even *be* wrong, and yet they will love you. There is a special soul connection with this kind of friend. Together, a shared vision and a shared destiny are possible. Robert South said, "A friend is a gift of God."[9]

FRIENDS OF GOD

All of us have been hurt, mistreated, disrespected, stabbed in the back, betrayed, and taken advantage of, but how do we respond to people who stand in opposition to what God has for us? Adam and Eve's relationship with God gives us some good direction on this. In response to His love for them, God dealt with Adam and Eve in love both before the Fall and after. As hard as it was for them to experience such a breach of trust, He still made a way for them to restore their relationship with Him and continue to walk in intimate agreement as they had done in the garden.

There is no way to measure the value of true friendships without understanding the energy and the wealth God has poured into making us His friends. God has chosen us to make us a gift to Himself, and friendship is the greatest treasure we can give or receive from another.

Let's look now at the qualities found in God's friendship with mankind.

Generosity

The first thing we learn about God is that He is a generous friend. He created a wonderful world for His friends. The Garden of Eden was a beautiful place where friendships could flourish. It was a place of intimacy and pleasure. God is always willing to bless His true friends and provide for them. A true friend spares no expense for someone he loves.

Encouragement

God is an encouragement to us all. He desires His friends to be successful. We see God's demonstration of encouragement to man through how He dealt with Adam and Eve. He encouraged them to be all He created them to be through His generosity in giving them everything, His words and companionship in the daily walks, and His clear warnings to them of dangers that lurked in their own souls. After their fall He loved them, covered them, and made a way for them to come home forgiven.

And even now with us, He has given us over three thousand promises in His Word in order to encourage us to reach our full potential. He says He loves us, believes in us, formed us, prays for us, died for us, and has gifted us with the gifts of His Spirit to accomplish the purpose He has for us. His Word teaches us that His love never fails, never runs out, and never changes. He will never leave us or forsake us, and He has given us His armor to fight against the opposition. He is coming back for us, and we ought to live life with a joyful expectation of His return.

Accountability

God requires accountability in friendship. God placed one restriction on His friends in the Garden of Eden in Genesis 2:16–17 (NIV):

> And the LORD God commanded the man, "You are free to eat from any tree in the garden; but you must not eat from the tree of the knowledge of good and evil, for when you eat of it you will surely die."

After all God had blessed Adam and Eve with, He asked His friends to refrain from eating from this one tree. In this moment He became their accountability partner.

In real friendships, we give others the right to ask the tough questions. Genuine relationships always hold each other accountable. A true friend will listen to you even if what you are saying hurts them. The Bible tells us that wounds from a friend can be trusted. (See Proverbs 27:6.)

Oftentimes we want people to agree with us or take our side, but a true friend will hold you accountable and try to help you see you're wrong in any given situation. A true friend should hold you accountable for your actions.

Trustworthiness

A friend ought to be trustworthy. God made man king of the earth and gave him stewardship over all its resources. Adam was in charge of naming all the animals and was responsible for their environment. A real friend can be trusted with anything. As I stated in the previous chapter, if they are telling other people's secrets to you, then you can bet your bottom dollar they are spreading your private information to other people.

Does God trust you? Do your friends trust you? Are you the first person they reveal things to, or the last? If God can't trust you with what you have, then why would He bless you with more? Same goes for your friends. If there is not a mutual trust, then your relationship will never grow into what God desires for you.

Security

A true friend desires that you enjoy the friendship of others. I remember growing up I had a friend who would get mad if I didn't tell him everything I was doing on the weekends and with whom I was doing it. He felt that because we were best friends he should automatically be included in everything that I did. The problem was, I had many different circles of friends, and I didn't like being around the same people all the time.

Most of the time, we see this attitude in extremely insecure people. Some are insecure and some struggle with a spirit of inferiority. An insecure person (much like the enemy) will attach himself to a mature person who cares for him and will use that relationship for personal gain. I have experienced much pain over the years from people who used me to further themselves. I have experienced this in athletics, community service, the corporate world, and in ministry.

God gave Eve to Adam. God wanted man to be complete, so He gave him a friend, helper, and lover. It would have been much easier for God to isolate Adam and keep him all to Himself, but He wanted what was best for Adam.

Some people would rather have you all to themselves rather than to see God bless you. Any relationship that isolates you from other people is unhealthy. This is defined as codependence. Instead of sharing mutual rewards, the relationship becomes one-sided and selfish.

Gratitude

So, how did Adam and Eve rate as friends? What was their response to the One who desired their companionship? They were ungrateful for what their divine Friend had brought to their lives. They could only focus on what they did not have rather than on what they had already been given. So many people will throw years of togetherness away for one minute of disagreement.

You may be one who has a friend or mentor who has poured his life and resources into you. Much of what you have become is because of their generosity and encouragement. Have you ever gone to that person unbidden, and just said to him, "You mean so much to my life. Thank you for loving me and believing in me"? Too often we fail to express gratitude, but this is an important trait in genuine friendship.

Loyalty

Adam and Eve also valued position and power more than their relationship with their Friend. Everything they had become was because of God. Yet the allure of power and position drew them away from their friendship with God. In the end, they sold out their truest Friend in a grab for power, much like Judas Iscariot when he betrayed Christ before His death.

This sad tale is repeated over and over again in our society. Those in position of great authority often find it difficult to distinguish friends from those trying to gain position and prestige. There is a question that you should ask about any partnership: "Is this person close to me because of who I am or because of what I do?" A real friend is not a user or a manipulator.

Adam and Eve further failed in their friendship with God when they valued the voice of a stranger more than the voice of their true Friend. They listened to the lies of the serpent over the voice of the God whom they had walked with day after day. It is interesting how many across the years have taken the opinion of people of questionable reputation over the wisdom of a real friend. Remember that the attractive words of a stranger may cloak the voice of Satan himself.

The most powerful and hurtful of all emotions is the pain of a friend's betrayal. Long before Judas sold out Jesus with a kiss, Adam and Eve embraced the serpent in the Garden of Eden. God was betrayed by those He loved the most.

Betrayal is not an option where there is a bond of love. The love of God creates that kind of powerful bond. Despite the way God's first human friends treated Him, He provided a way for all those who wanted His friendship to approach

Him without fear. Echoing through the Old Testament are the plaintive cries of the heart of God:

> Fear not, for I have redeemed you; I have summoned you by name; you are mine.
>
> —ISAIAH 43:1, NIV

> With everlasting kindness I will have compassion on you...
>
> —ISAIAH 54:8, NIV

> I have loved you with an everlasting love...
>
> —JEREMIAH 31:3

> When Israel was a child, I loved him, and out of Egypt I called My son.
>
> —HOSEA 11:1

> How can I give you up, Ephraim?...
>
> —HOSEA 11:8, NIV

> Call unto me, and I will answer you...
>
> —JEREMIAH 33:3

God would pay the ultimate price of love by dying to bring His friends home. We must forgive those friends who have hurt us and move forward with God and others. We must learn to be generous to our friends, encouraging them when they are down, holding ourselves accountable to them when we make mistakes, and being responsible with the task given to us by our friends. We must learn to serve our friends unselfishly and be grateful for what they have done for us. Repeat these prayers after me:

Prayer for you if you have been hurt by your friends:

Lord, I forgive (name the friends who hurt you in your past) for what they did to me. Please loose me from my past so I can move forward into my future with You. Please take away my pain, hurt, and anger. I lay my emotions at Your feet, and I surrender my life to You.

Prayer for you if you haven't been a godly friend:

Lord, please forgive me for my (selfishness, ungratefulness, discouragement, and dishonor) toward my friend. Please forgive me for my wrong spirit toward this person. I ask You to make in me a clean heart, O God. I ask that You bless my friend in abundance, favor, and grace. In Jesus's name, amen.

Chapter 11

WHAT KEEPS US FROM WALKING IN AGREEMENT WITH OTHERS?

By Ronnie Phillips Jr.

T HROUGHOUT THE PAGES of Holy Scripture a war rages against humanity! Satan's strategy then and now is to divide and conquer. As we noted in the last chapter, this breach first happens to Adam and Eve and costs them the paradise of Eden. This disunity and broken relationship continues through the dark history of humanity. All the wars, the deaths, and the heartaches flow from that broken trust.

Satan has released demonic forces that rage against the unity in the body of Christ that Jesus died and rose again to give us. Before we unpack the biblical model for miracle relationships, let us be sure we recognize the demons that oppose the kind of agreement that releases the supernatural.

When you trek through the pages of Scripture, you confront a number of dark spirits that hinder God-sized unity, agreement, and connections.

Cain: the spirit of jealousy

First, beware of the spirit of Cain. This spirit is clearly jealousy. This spirit moved through Cain against his brother, Abel, over position in worship. Interestingly, Cain killed his brother in the field at harvest time. (See Genesis 4:8.)

There is a principle for us to learn here from Genesis 4. The enemy comes to bring death to your dreams right before God is about to fulfill them. The enemy comes to divide us and what ends up happening is that neither person experiences all that God has for him. The spirit of jealousy ruins relationships, and it kills agreement within the body of Christ. Satan knows if he can divide brothers in church, he can hinder worship and the harvest of souls and blessing. This spirit always kills!

Ham: the spirit of dishonor

Second, watch out for the spirit of Ham. This second-born son of Noah uncovered his father's nakedness. (See Genesis 9:20–25.) This is the spirit of dishonor. Today it manifests itself in those who betray confidential information about someone who trusts them. To spread bad reports about other Christians will bring a curse of dishonor on an individual and his family. (See Exodus 21:17; Leviticus 20:9; Proverbs 6:16–19; 20:20; Matthew 15:4; Ephesians 6:1–3.)

Esau: the spirit of bitterness

Third, the spirit of Esau is the most destructive of all spirits when it comes to doing life together. Scripture says:

> Pursue peace with all people, and holiness, without which no one will see the Lord: looking carefully lest anyone fall short of the grace of God; lest any root of

bitterness springing up cause trouble, and by this many become defiled; lest there be any fornicator or pro-fane person like Esau, who for one morsel of food sold his birthright. For you know that afterward, when he wanted to inherit the blessing, he was rejected, for he found no place for repentance, though he sought it dili-gently with tears.

—Hebrews 12:14–17

Esau became bitter as this spirit divided his family. His descendants were the Edomites, a cursed people. Bitterness gives evidence of an unforgiving spirit. The root of bitterness grows into a tree of offense and defies the lives of many.

Saul: the spirit of paranoia

Sadly, we look next at the spirit of Saul. Saul had a spirit of paranoia that led to extreme depression. Saul went mad because the throne had become more important to him than the task. A good leader embraces the next generation and is not threatened by their talent or the calling God has placed on them. We learn that Saul and his son died in battle, so the spirit of paranoia was a distraction that kept them off course. Saul ran off David, who viewed him as a father. Saul's heavi-ness led to the destruction of his family.

You must embrace the success of others. Insecurity leads to paranoia. Paranoia leads to destruction.

Rehoboam: the spirit of pride

Solomon's son, Rehoboam, had a spirit of pride that refused to give honor and attention to his elders. (See 1 Kings 12.) His actions divided Israel into two nations and set them on a course to captivity. (See 2 Chronicles 10.) Proverbs 16:5 says, "Everyone proud in heart is an abomination to the Lord;

145

though they join forces, none will go unpunished." This spirit still leads to bondage and broken relationships.

Ahab and Jezebel: the spirit of control

Look at the spirits of Ahab and Jezebel. Jezebel had the spirit of control. This spirit manipulates and destroys quality friendships because one person tries to control every decision the other person makes. Friendships are built out of love, loyalty, and acceptance. Control is acceptance based on only one person's terms. Genuine relationships are about love, not control.

Ahab suffered from a codependent spirit that allowed Jezebel to rob the nation and destroy his reign as king. A codependent spirit is a spirit where one person is trying to make the relationship flourish, constantly trying to please the other person and win his approval, but the other person is not easily won nor is he putting the same effort into the relationship. This brings frustration, unhappiness, bitterness, and resentment.

We have all had that friend who always expects us to be there for him but has never been there when we needed him. Break away from this spirit and allow the Holy Spirit to lead you toward the right people.

Ahab and Jezebel would both die untimely deaths, cursed by bad relationships. Don't let this be how you are remembered.

Gomer: the spirit of seduction, harlotry, and lust

Notice also the spirit of Gomer found in the Book of Hosea. Gomer left her husband, committed adultery, became a temple prostitute, and finally a slave. She was restored by the love of her husband, Hosea.

This spirit is the spirit of seduction, harlotry, and lust. This spirit uses sex to bring iniquity and shame. Sexual failure destroys quality relationships.

Job's friends: the religious spirit

In Job's friends Eliphaz, Bildad, and Zophar we observe the religious spirit, the legalistic spirit, and the spirit of this age. All are deceptive and destructive. Job's friends were too busy judging him and acting religious to show Christian compassion to him during his trials. They basically said in Job chapter 4 that it was all his fault that he was experiencing loss and was struggling. So many Christians are too busy trying to act spiritual and give religious answers that they miss opportunities to minister to those who are in real need of a friend.

Judas Iscariot and Demas: the spirit of betrayal

In Judas Iscariot and Demas we observe the spirit of betrayal. There is nothing more hurtful and destructive to friendships than betrayal. Demas betrayed Paul and broke his heart when he needed him most. Demas stood by Paul as he preached the gospel of Jesus Christ. Paul was beaten, left for dead, and imprisoned for what he preached. Demas had been there for most of it. There are friends for a reason, a season, and very few for a lifetime. Demas had a love for the present world, so he departed. (See 2 Timothy 4:10.) Many of us have experienced betrayal, but thank God there is a friend who sticks closer than a brother (Prov. 18:24).

Elymas: the spirit of manipulation

In Acts 13 we see the spirit of Elymas, who was a sorcerer. He tried to buy the anointing of the Holy Spirit. He wanted to manipulate others with his phony spiritual power. This spirit of manipulation is observed today in those who would use their friendships to gain personal advantage.

Being the son of a well-known Southern Baptist pastor has been both a blessing and at times has felt like a curse. All during my childhood people would want to be close to me because of who my dad was. Adults would befriend me so they could use it to gain some power in our church or get close to my father. As a pastor myself, I now see people who want to be friends with me for the wrong reasons. Manipulation makes people feel dirty, unwanted, and unworthy. May the Lord give you the discernment to see who your real friends are.

Let us be warned about these demons that hinder the agreement in relationships. Unity in relationships is the key that unlocks heaven.

These are all biblical examples of what keep us from walking in agreement with others. We must combat pride with humility (Ps. 149:4). We must combat bitterness with love (Matt. 5:44). We must combat paranoia with a renewed mind (Rom. 12:1–2). We must combat control with faith in God (Rom. 5:1–5). We must combat lust with His righteousness (Matt. 6:33). We must combat the religious spirit with grace. Grace is the key to warfare. You must know of His grace. Grow in grace and show others this grace. Don't be so hard on people and God won't be so hard on you. (See Colossians 4:5-6.)

The Bible says in Isaiah 48:22, "'There is no peace,' says the LORD, 'for the wicked.'" If you don't have peace and have trouble walking in agreement with others, then first you need to understand that your battle is not with these individuals. It is with the enemy, according to Ephesians 6:12.

To begin to walk in freedom from the things that keep you

in disagreement, pray this prayer and ask God to deliver you from all unrighteousness.

> *Dear Lord, forgive me for waging war against other people. I know my battle is not with them but with the enemy. Give me the strength and the power to wage war against the enemy.*
>
> *Satan, you are a liar, a murderer, and a thief. You have been defeated by the blood of Jesus Christ. I choose to walk in victory today. I choose to forgive those who have hurt me and move forward with my life. In Jesus's name, Amen.*

Chapter 12

THE HIDDEN POWER
OF SUBMISSION

By Ronnie Phillips Jr.

C. S. Lewis, author of *The Lion, the Witch and the Wardrobe*, once said, "Don't be scared by the word *authority*."[1] But nothing causes more friction in the Western world than submitting to authority. First Timothy 2:1–6 (NIV) says:

> I urge, then, first of all, that requests, prayers, intercession and thanksgiving be made for everyone—for kings and all those in authority, that we may live peaceful and quiet lives in all godliness and holiness. This is good, and pleases God our Savior, who wants all men to be saved and to come to a knowledge of the truth. For there is one God and one mediator between God and men, the man Christ Jesus, who gave himself as a ransom for all men—the testimony given in its proper time.

Paul explains that we are to pray for those who have been placed in charge of our lives and that it is pleasing to God. Hebrews 13:17 (ESV) makes it even more plain:

> Obey your leaders and submit to them, for they are keeping watch over your souls, as those who will have to give an account. Let them do this with joy and not with groaning, for that would be of no advantage to you.

Some of the most talented and gifted men and women in the church world fail to see the connection between obedience and pleasing God. Cheating on your taxes, speeding, and even littering isn't exercising your opinion or making a statement; it's displeasing to God, and it is rebellion. First Samuel 15:23 says that rebellion is the same as witchcraft. Not following the instruction, correction, and advice of your pastor isn't just a disagreement; it is rebellion.

This is difficult for our modern culture, because as an institution increases in its size, power, and influence, it is seen as "the Man," a term from the 1950s to mean warden or jailer. So we have grown accustomed to celebrating those who defy authority. Here in America we celebrate our Declaration of Independence every July. We sing songs and watch explosions in the sky, commemorating a time in history when a group of people refused to be silenced and challenged the greatest army on earth—and won!

We celebrate rebellion in fiction as well. Who can forget the Rebel Alliance in George Lucas's classic, *Star Wars*? Here, the Rebel Alliance challenges the evil rule of Darth Vader and the Emperor. A space fight, saber fight, and several hundred billion dollars later, the Rebel Alliance wins!

Americans love pulling for "the underdog." Think about

all of the literature and movies that celebrate challenging authority. It's in our cultural DNA to question and challenge our leadership.

There is still a sense of pride that swells in the Southern states of America when we discuss the Civil War, or as referred to by some Southerners, "the War of Northern Aggression." Only the Bible has been printed more than literature on the Civil War, as the discussion and debates continue well over a hundred years after the war's conclusion.

But there is only one biblical mandate for rebellion in the Bible. Acts 5:29 says, "We must obey God rather than men!" (NIV). The only reason to rebel against authority is if obedience to God is in question. While one may justify his actions or thoughts using the Bible, this scripture should stand as a test in determining if one is in rebellion. Think of all the people whom God has placed over us in authority. These are the people God has placed in position to assist you on your quest. These leaders are not against you; they are in your fellowship. At times, they provide guidelines or parameters for your quest, but most of all, they provide safety.

A staff member who used to work in our church's maintenance department told me something interesting: "You can always tell people who have issues with authority." I asked him how that was possible, and he said, "Because wherever I hang signs that say DO NOT WALK for their own safety, people with authority issues walk *there* anyway." That may sound too extreme, but you have to ask yourself why someone would walk where they are told not to walk, knowing that the signs are placed there for safety reasons. In essence, the person who defies the rules defies his own safety and well-being.

While it's more than just a legalistic list, here are a few

examples of people God may have placed in your life to give you the accountability and guidance you need to fulfill your purpose:

- Parents
- Grandparents
- Pastors
- Teachers
- Deacons
- Police
- Fire department
- Military officials
- Elected officials

Even Jesus, King of kings, and Lord of lords, obeyed earthly authorities. Jesus paid His taxes!

> Keeping a close watch on him, they sent spies, who pretended to be honest. They hoped to catch Jesus in something he said so that they might hand him over to the power and authority of the governor. So the spies questioned him: "Teacher...is it right for us to pay taxes to Caesar or not?" He saw through their duplicity and said to them, "Show me a denarius. Whose portrait and inscription are on it?" "Caesar's," they replied. He said to them, "Then give to Caesar what is Caesar's, and to God what is God's."
>
> —LUKE 20:20–25, NIV

Submission Helps You Conquer Your Quest

J. R. R. Tolkien began developing his characters for *The Hobbit* and *The Lord of the Rings* universe in the trenches of World War I. The destruction of nature and battlefield atrocities filled Tolkien's young mind with terror and forced Tolkien to invent an allegorical world through his vivid imagination. In this fictional world, Tolkien tells a story of good triumphing over evil. It is not by coincidence that Tolkien makes friendship or fellowship the centerpiece of his stories. Tolkien saw firsthand that winning battles as well as adventures is only possible when we are in fellowship.[2]

Tolkien's characters are finally developed when their destiny is accepted, but the pursuit of this destiny is impossible without the help of the others. I am reminded of Bilbo Baggins. This character wants a "simple" life, boasting at one point that "nothing unexpected ever happened."[3] But after receiving some strange visitors, he finds himself on a life-changing adventure. Bilbo's fictional quest to assist in fighting an evil dragon gives him maturity and wisdom, and changes his mind-set and destiny forever.

Bilbo has to learn his position or place in the fellowship and how to operate under the authority of Thorin Oakenshield, the pompous leader. Bilbo and Thorin realize that they need each other to achieve their destiny of defeating the dragon.[4]

We too are invited on a quest, and we must learn to operate effectively with those whom God has placed beside us and behind us, and those who lead us. Like Bilbo, we are often surrounded with people we would never expect.

God longs for us to learn from one another, serve one another, and love one another. It was never His plan for us to stick to people who do whatever we say and do, who are on the same level as we are and never challenge us to grow. We must understand the power of being able to follow someone else's leadership or direction and help him achieve his destiny on the road to achieving ours. This is the fellowship Christ intended for His people.

A Lesson in Submission from Judas

We must look at the story of Judas Iscariot to examine some of the potential pitfalls you can face when your teammate, employee, or business acquaintance is in it for their own personal gain and not yours as the leader.

Judas Iscariot was and will forever be known as the one who betrayed Jesus. His story teaches us about the dark side of failing to submit to authority and in turn falling out of fellowship with other believers. Judas started out as Jesus's friend, but what happened? We know that Judas was the treasurer who handled the money for the ministry of the twelve, so Jesus had trusted him in the beginning. Jesus gave Judas His full confidence that he would help carry out the vision for His ministry by managing the funds. But I believe the power and prestige went to his head. Power is a strange thing. Oftentimes, power will turn a humble servant into a prideful slave to the enemy.

In Matthew 26 we can begin to see the signs of Judas's rebellion as he responded angrily to the woman who came into the house of Simon the Leper and poured the alabaster flask of very costly oil on the head of Jesus. He questioned her worship of Jesus by saying, "Why this waste?" This tells me that Judas ultimately doubted that Jesus was even worthy of such worship. If he had the faith that Jesus really was the Son of God, I doubt that he would have seen this woman's lavish display as wasteful. There are a few other things this account reveals about Judas and his lack of submission to authority.

1. Judas had lost his love for his leader.

The business had gotten in the way of his love for his Leader—the One who entrusted him and promoted him. We must never forget where we came from and the people who helped get us there. Judas had forgotten what was really important, and that was Christ and His ministry. There are times when people lose heart, faith, and the ability to support the vision of their leader. This can lead to division and disunity—an open door for the enemy to come in and disrupt the fellowship.

2. Judas had begun to negatively influence the group.

I believe Judas was the one who was most upset in Matthew 26, but the Bible leads us to believe that many of the disciples were bothered by this event. This means that the negative spirit of Judas had temporarily spread to the other disciples. Sometimes it is best to keep our opinions to ourselves when God is doing something in our midst.

Jesus responds to His disciples in the form of a rebuke. He says to them in Matthew 26:10–12, "Why are you bothering this woman? She has done a beautiful thing to me. The poor you will always have with you, but you will not always have me. When she poured this perfume on my body, she did it to prepare me for burial" (NIV).

There are many times when we may not agree with the person God has placed above us. Many of us have to deal with these things internally and discern what God is trying to teach us during those times. Sometimes we may be right, but God is still teaching us to submit, learn, and grow into the leader He has called us to be. It is possible to stay submissive and learn from the mistakes of others, but my experience is that usually the leader has a different perspective than I do.

The failure was how Judas responded to this rebuke. Judas was finished with Jesus. I imagine that he had had enough of Him and felt like he would get what was his. Judas must have thought that he was going to turn Jesus in to the chief priests, get his thirty pieces of silver, start a new life, and just focus on his own destiny. He must have been tired of being the second man, and he refused to live his life in the shadows of his leader.

ARE YOU IN AGREEMENT WITH THOSE IN AUTHORITY OVER YOU?

The reason famous musical groups break up, marriages end in divorce, friendships end, churches split, and businesses fail is because people are unwilling to submit to the governing authorities God has placed above them. We all pass judgment on Judas, but many of us live our lives in a very similar way. We are disgruntled and selfish and think we know more than our leader. This does happen sometimes when we don't keep a check on our hearts, but thank God for the Holy Spirit. We need to ask God to show us where we are off. He will help us get back on track. Self-examination guided by the Holy Spirit is wise so that we don't ruin the God-connections in our lives.

Here are some signs that you may not be in unity with your leader:

1. You feel as though your agenda is more important than your leader's.

Are you an undercover self-promoter? Does every idea or suggestion benefit you first and the leader's agenda a far second? I worked for a Fortune 500 insurance company for seven years prior to starting in ministry, and I learned from the mistakes of my peers that a sure way to get terminated was to be building a website or promoting your own business while on the company's time. This goes on too often in churches around America.

2. The quality of your work or faithfulness to your leader begins to falter.

In the case of Judas, money was missing. Everyone hits a dry spell or a season when he is not at his best. If there are personal issues, offenses, or frustrations that are causing you to see your leader in a different light, set time aside with your leader to communicate these things with respect and love. But do not seek to control or manipulate him.

3. You question your leader's decisions in front of other people or behind his back.

It is appropriate to question your leaders in a professional and private manner. Your leader needs mature and quality people around him who will come to him privately and respectfully and ask the tough questions. This is completely acceptable. But do not criticize your leader publicly or to other members of the fellowship.

4. You isolate yourself from your leader and the other team members.

Judas was sneaking off to the chief priests, having private meetings, and misappropriating funds. Leaders can't effectively operate in the place that God has anointed them to if they never see you. God has anointed your leader in a special way that can grow the areas of your life that need maturity. The right connection between you and your leader is a powerful alliance—one the enemy desperately seeks to pollute with pride and rebellion. Do not isolate yourself; do not give the enemy a chance to plant negative seeds in your mind. Bring to light the things that may cause you to feel like withdrawing by addressing them with your leader. These things can be resolved in love, honor, and respect.

If these four things aren't dealt with immediately, they can lead to a betrayal or deep wound to you and a detour in your journey to destiny.

FIVE BENEFITS OF LIVING A LIFE UNDER AUTHORITY

Jesus placed relationship over assignment. He even did everything in His power to restore Judas after he had betrayed Him. Jesus was not the lone ranger. His anointing was accompanied by His relationship with the people around Him. If you look at the twelve disciples you will see a variety of gifts, personalities, and cultures. All of them were different, but that is what made the New Testament leaders so effective. We must embrace one another's various gifts and positions in the kingdom, submitting to one another as we submit to Christ. There is a commanded blessing that comes on our lives when we are open to learning from one another, preferring one another, and receiving help from one another:

1. You'll live a higher life.

It's a matter of purpose; it's the longing of something more. Many of us are stuck in depressed and boring routines, a joyless grind we call a life. A higher life involves having a purpose on earth, a purpose that matches the gifts that God has given you as an individual. People say there is no greater purpose that brings more joy to one's soul than serving Jesus Christ. There is a purpose greater and that is serving Jesus Christ as an individual with the gifts God has given you! It does no good to live someone else's dream.

It's a matter of position. Christ is seated at the right hand of God and Romans 6 tells us that we are alive with Christ. What that means is that each one of our lives plays a role in the position of Jesus because we are His children for whom He died.

> In the same way, count yourselves dead to sin but alive to God in Christ Jesus. Therefore do not let sin reign in your mortal body so that you obey its evil desires. Do not offer the parts of your body to sin, as instruments of wickedness, but rather offer yourselves to God, as those who have been brought from death to life; and offer the parts of your body to him as instruments of righteousness. For sin shall not be your master, because you are not under law, but under grace.
> —ROMANS 6:11–14, NIV

It is also a matter of practice. Christians aren't perfect, but as a matter of practice a Christian talks, serves, and loves God. It doesn't mean Christians don't get sick, don't sin, don't die early, but what it does mean is that we have a coping mechanism. We know to whom we must take our problems. Not to the world and worldly advice and copping behaviors and habits, but to Jesus Christ. The Christian life is a higher life because of our purpose, our position in Christ, and our practice.

2. You'll live a secure life or hidden life.

Colossians 3:3–4 says, "For you died, and your life is now hidden with Christ in God. When Christ who is your life appears, then you also will appear with Him in glory."

This refers to the security we have as Christians. I tell you there is security in Christ Jesus our Lord and Savior. There is a knowing when you are walking with the Lord. John 10:27–29 (NIV) says:

> My sheep listen to my voice; I know them, and they follow me. I give them eternal life, and they shall never perish; no one can snatch them out of my hand. My Father, who has given them to me, is greater than all; no one can snatch them out of my Father's hand.

If you have truly submitted your life to Christ as your Lord and Savior then no power of hell can snatch you out of God's hand. You are hidden in God's hand.

Some people say you can lose your salvation; I believe if you truly have it then you can't lose it. The problem is that some folks don't truly have it, or they have drifted off. If you are saved then you are hidden with Christ and you are abiding in Christ, and no power of the enemy, no fleshly mistake can snatch you out of God's hand. Can you turn your back on

God? Can you sin? Absolutely, but God will always be there to welcome you back in His arms.

3. You'll live a holy life.

A sure way to tell if a person is living a life of submission is to examine his lifestyle. Colossians 3:5–8 says, "Put to death, therefore, whatever belongs to your earthly nature: sexual immorality, impurity, lust, evil desires and greed, which is idolatry. Because of these, the wrath of God is coming. You used to walk in these ways, in the life you once lived. But now you must rid yourselves of all such things as these: anger, rage, malice, slander, and filthy language from your lips" (NIV).

The world calls this behavior normal, but our walk with Christ should change these human attributes and lead us to live a holy life.

4. You'll live a heavenly life.

A life under authority means that you are under the authority of Jesus Christ. Matthew 28:18 says, "Then Jesus came to them and said, 'All authority in heaven and on earth has been given to me'" (NIV). This divine authority has the power to change our surroundings, our finances, our friendships, and our destiny.

> The Spirit of the Lord has been given to me, for he has anointed me. He has sent me to bring the good news to the poor, to proclaim liberty to captives and to the blind new sight, to set the downtrodden free.
> —LUKE 4:18, NJB

And this divine power is given to those who are living life under authority.

When Jesus had called the Twelve together, he gave them power and authority to drive out all demons and to cure diseases, and he sent them out to preach the kingdom of God and to heal the sick.

—LUKE 9:1–2, NIV

The seventy-two returned with joy and said, "Lord, even the demons submit to us in your name." He replied, "I saw Satan fall like lightning from heaven. I have given you authority to trample on snakes and scorpions and to overcome all the power of the enemy; nothing will harm you. However, do not rejoice that the spirits submit to you, but rejoice that your names are written in heaven."

—LUKE 10:17–20, NIV

There is great power given to those who choose to defy the worldly perception of rebellion and live a life under authority.

5. You'll live an honored life.

An honored life is a life that has been lived under authority as an example to the next generation of believers. How many believers have squandered a place of honor, power, dignity, and respect for sinful pleasures that last but moments in time? An honored life is a life that not only lends itself in servanthood but also challenges the next generation.

I think of my father when I think of an honored life. I think of the thousands of people who are touched by his ministry—a ministry that was built by God with integrity, character, and grace. I think of the thousands of people whose lives are forever changed because my father is able to finish what he started so many years ago. When I think of an honored life I think of a sermon my father preached a few years ago. In the sermon he said he was asked, "How did you grow a mega-church?" His reply, "I stayed."

My father stayed the course through abusive church members and typical family hardships. Dad stayed despite lucrative offers to leave. He stayed and is finishing his destiny with dignity and honor. In 2 Timothy 4:7–8 the apostle Paul is finishing his ministry and declares that has finished the race with honor and dignity:

> I have fought the good fight, I have finished the race, I have kept the faith. Now there is in store for me the crown of righteousness, which the Lord, the righteous Judge, will award to me on that day—and not only to me, but also to all who have longed for his appearing.
>
> —NIV

Chapter 13

DYNAMIC CONNECTIONS: THE JESUS MODEL

By Ronnie Phillips Jr.

IT IS NO secret that friendships come and go. My wife always tells me that there are friends for a reason, friends for a season, and friends for a lifetime. In other words, some relationships are more meaningful than others.

This truth may be most strongly apparent to any family who has hosted a slumber party attended by an active pack of little girls or boys. The sleeping bags and pillows are barely inside the front door before a pairing off of buddies occurs! Little Jill and Molly have known each other since preschool, and they are soon socializing over the interest they share. Tina and Megan are in the same ballet class and become busy sharing their newest skills with each other. Unfortunately, Erin and Susie are fairly new to the area and so find themselves thrown together by default. Their predicament and insecurity is their bond. People call these things "cliques."

The same basic dynamics that set childhood friendships in motion are present in our adult lives. Time, circumstances, values, and interests all play a part in the development of divine connections on multiple levels. God ultimately leads those who follow Him into a common destiny with others.

Common destiny is what strengthens the bonds in the dynamic relationships I believe God has designed for us as we journey through this life. Jesus showed us what kinds of supernatural things can happen when you align yourself with the right people—people who share your same interest, call, or destiny in life. He and His disciples accomplished uncommon tasks and worked unheard of miracles—together. They ate together, talked together, laughed together, and lived everyday life together. Jesus's disciples became His extended family, His kindred.

In Jesus's ministry His relationships and friendships preceded ministry. The disciples' first function was to be Jesus's friend, to be His companions. (See John 15:12–14.) Perhaps the greatest failure of the disciples was at Gethsemane when Jesus needed them most. In their fleshly weakness, they left Him alone in His darkest hours.

If the Son of God needed friends He could count on, then certainly we do! If friendship was a priority with Jesus, then you should be sensitive to that need as well. In the end God's creative power is released in the partnership of "soul mates." These friendships extend beyond time into eternity.

Most of us keep ourselves so busy and numb with activity that we do not realize how lonely we can be. Jesus is the model friend. He is the friend who sticks closer than a brother. Before you can be a friend, you need to make friends with Jesus.

What kind of friend is He? What patterns did He set forth for friendship?

JESUS LOVED HIS FRIENDS
THE WAY THEY WERE

The disciple who loved Jesus carefully penned the words of His Master:

> "My command is this: Love each other as I have loved you. Greater love has no one than this, that he lay down his life for his friends. You are my friends if you do what I command. I no longer call you servants, because a servant does not know his master's business. Instead, I have called you friends, for everything that I learned from my Father I have made known to you. You did not choose me, but I chose you and appointed you to go and bear fruit—fruit that will last. Then the Father will give you whatever you ask in my name. This is my command: Love each other. If the world hates you, keep in mind that it hated me first. If you belonged to the world, it would love you as its own. As it is, you do not belong to the world, but I have chosen you out of the world. That is why the world hates you."
>
> —JOHN 15:12–19, NIV

Agape love is the godly type of love and is the basis for all real friendship. Love must be willing to serve the other person.

In Job's tragedy, three so-called friends show up, but they could not love Job in his broken condition. "Then they sat down on the ground with him....No one said a word to him, because they saw how great his suffering was" (Job 2:13, NIV). A real friend loves a person when he is in pain. David echoes the pain of Job in Psalm 41:9, "Even my close friend, whom I trusted, he who shared my bread, has lifted up his heel against me." How often those whom we think are our friends turn away when trouble comes!

People can be bound together in the love of friendship when they gain the ability to be real in each other's presence. Ralph Waldo Emerson has said, "It is one of the blessings of old friends that you can afford to be stupid with them."[1] Love sympathizes, forgives, and laughs out loud with real friends. Proverbs 17:17 states, "A friend loves at all times." A true friend will love you at your best and at your worst.

JESUS SHARED HIS DEEPEST SECRETS WITH HIS FRIENDS

> I no longer call you servants, because a servant does not know his master's business. Instead, I have called you friends, for everything that I learned from my father I have made known to you.
>
> —JOHN 15:15

"I'm going to tell you some secrets!" This is what Jesus said when He came to earth. "I'm going to tell you what the Father is talking about, because we are friends. I am going to let you in on what is going on." With a real friend, you can share those deepest secrets of your heart, and he won't betray you.

The lesson some have never learned—which, sadly, has cost them their closest friends—is that you don't tell your friends' confidences. Betrayal of a confidence is one of the most common causes of broken friendships.

One of the first people in Scripture to be called God's friend was Abraham. In his friendship with God, he held nothing back from Him, not even his beloved son Isaac. Because of Abraham's faith, God held nothing back from His servant. He gave Abraham a country and a destiny. Then, disaster looms on the horizon as God decides He must nuke Sodom and Gomorrah. Within the city lived Lot, the nephew of Abraham. In Genesis 18:17, God exclaims from His heart, "Shall I hide from Abraham what I am about to do?" (NIV). God decided to call Abraham and tell him what was about to happen, although He told no one else on the face of the planet.

A friend is someone to whom you tell your hardest, most difficult secret and he won't betray you. Do you know how many people in our world are desperate to know they have just one person to count on? You say, "I really would like to have a friend like that." You must first *be* a loyal friend in order to *have* a loyal friend. That is why He said, "A man that hath friends must shew himself friendly" (Prov. 18:24, KJV).

Whom do you have that you can trust with anything you have, and he could trust you with the same? A true friend will not hold back from those he loves.

JESUS ENCOURAGED HIS FRIENDS TO REACH THEIR FULLEST POTENTIAL

In John 15:16, Jesus set forth the potential of real friendship: "You did not choose Me, but I chose you and appointed you that you should go and bear fruit, and that your fruit should remain, that whatever you ask the Father in My name He may give you." In essence, He said, "Our relationship together is going to make you a better person." You ought to engage in friendship that lifts you up, not pulls you down.

No doubt you've experienced the uncomfortable sense that

each time you are walking away from someone whom you consider a friend, you feel worse than you did when you first walked up to him. That is not a true friend. You are more likely in a codependent relationship with that individual. That means there will be some fire, some spark in your relationship, and you'll be a sharper person because you hang around that person. There are those who cannot grow on the job or in the church because they are hanging around losers who refuse to do anything but gripe or whine.

You must find some friends who can help you go where God wants you to go. Real friends are an encouragement. Oliver Wendell Holmes said, "Except in cases of necessity, which are rare, leave your friend to learn unpleasant things from his enemies; they are ready enough to tell them."[2] Be the encourager. Have you ever read the verse from Proverbs, "Faithful are the wounds of a friend" (Prov. 27:6, KJV)? You thought, "Well, buddy, I'll just punch my friend up a bit and straighten him out; that's what the verse means." Wrong answer! The word *faithful* there is not the normal use of the word. It is the phrase "to nurse" as a mother would breast-feed a child. Who has ever seen a mother slap her child while she was breast-feeding him? She comforts the crying children with her tender touch and precious words, "Honey, it's all right!" You must understand, the child thinks he is going to starve to death. He doesn't understand the sensations he is feeling in his tiny tummy. A mother simply murmurs, "Honey, it will be all right. Mother is right here. Everything is going to be OK." That is what the wound of a friend is. It is when the friend steps up, even when you may be wrong, and says, "It is going to be all right." They go ahead and give you whatever it takes to nourish you while correcting you gently.

Jesus Was a Friend People Could Talk To

Can you imagine a conversation with Jesus? He came with a joyful expression. He said, "I have spoken to you to give you joy. I want My joy to remain in you. I've come to fill you with joy." What friend do you have, where just seeing his face lights you up? I mean, when he walks into a room you start grinning because you are glad to see him. He is glad to see you, not a word being spoken, just a glance. That connection, that relationship, just bridges all gaps, and it is a joy to be with that person.

Proverbs 27:9 expresses this idea so beautifully. "Perfume and incense bring joy to the heart, and the pleasantness of one's friend springs from his [hearty] earnest counsel" (NIV). That word *hearty* is the Hebrew word *nephesh*. This is the same word used when God breathed into Adam, making him a *nephesh*, or a living soul. So the verse could read, "Ointment and perfume rejoice the heart. So does the sweetness of man's friend by his life-giving words." In other words, your words become life to your friend, not death to the spirit.

Jesus Sacrificed for the Sake of Friendship

> Greater love has no man than this, that he lay down his life for his friends.
>
> —John 15:13, NIV

Jesus looked out into space and time and we were friendless and hopeless, but He said, "I want them to be My friends." The Father replied, "They cannot be Your friends forever, because they are sinners." Jesus said, "What will it take for them to be My friends forever?" The Father sadly said, "You would have to die for them." So Jesus let them take Him out, and they beat Him and whipped Him. They crowned Him with thorns. They pierced His hands, His side, and His feet, and He cried out in the loneliness of that hour, "My God, My God, why have You forsaken Me?" He went through all that suffering so that He could say, "I want to be your friend."

JESUS WAS A FRIEND WHO WAS REAL ABOUT COMMUNICATION

A real friendship is a friendship that communicates. Christ sacrificed everything for this communication, and His sacrifice granted us a blessing to have "life...to the full" (John 10:10, NIV, see also 1 Pet. 1:3; 2 Cor. 5:17–6:2).

HOW CAN WE BE FRIENDS LIKE JESUS WAS?

There is no reason to chase codependent friendships or unhealthy and abusive relationships. You will not find the answers to life in the eyes of another person, and that person will not find all of the answers to life in you. There is only one Savior and His name is Jesus. Jesus said that *He* was the way, the truth, and the life (John 14:6). Despite popular literature that argues otherwise, Christ is the One who heals our broken hearts. You can't fix yourself, and if you can't fix yourself, you can't fix other people. Leave all the "fixing" to Jesus. A friendship that follows Christ's example is one that leads both individuals to seek the face of God, pointing each other toward the throne room of heaven—iron sharpening iron.

A great way to improve our earthly relationships is to improve our heavenly relationship with the Father. Jesus always maintained close contact with the Father. There's something transforming about spending time with God every day. So many times we see prayer as something to do at church or in the car on the way to school or work, and that time with God is important too. But like any relationship, God enjoys our company. When we set aside time just for Him, there are priceless rewards of rejuvenation, divine revelation, and heavenly information. During our time of intimate conversation with our Father, our minds are reset. The apostle Paul called this a "renewing of the mind" (Rom. 12:2).

This is how we defeat the ugliness that so often creeps into our friendships, like jealousy, lies, covetousness, paranoia, insecurity, inferiority, and strife, just to name a few. If you have ever watched television you will quickly learn what the world calls "normal" the Bible calls sin. On television we are taught that the above-mentioned things are normal in friendships. But you really can have friendships that are void of all the drama. Our church drama ministry has a saying, "Keep the drama on the stage!"

Through Christ's relationship with the disciples and His heavenly Father, we see the necessity of good communication in our relationships. It's normal for people to disagree and even argue. But we have to move past the point where we want to assign blame. How many times have you been in an argument with a friend or even your spouse only to spend most of the time assigning blame? In any argument, both parties are probably at fault. Dr. Ira Byock, head of Life's End Institute, gives us four phrases that bring healing to relationships:[3]

1. Please forgive me.

2. I forgive you.

3. Thank you.

4. I love you.

Learning to incorporate these four phrases into our normal vocabulary is not only helpful in our godly relationships, but it is necessary in maintaining a reputable walk with Christ.

Chapter 14

GENUINE AGREEMENT

By Ronnie Phillips Jr.

I BELIEVE THERE ARE relationships that put us in "lift off" mode. These relationships help us get on the right path, stay on the right path, and move around the earth with purpose. Jesus experienced these kinds of relationships. The apostle Paul knew of this union. Solomon, the wisest man who ever lived, saw the value of genuine relationships. Solomon described this union in Ecclesiastes 4:9–12 (NIV):

> Two are better than one, because they have a good return for their labor:
> If either of them falls down, one can help the other up. But pity anyone who falls and has no one to help them up. Also, if two lie down together, they will keep warm. But how can one keep warm alone? Though one may be overpowered, two can defend themselves. A cord of three strands is not quickly broken.

In your pursuit of God's path, you will discover that you are not alone on your journey. Not only is the Lord with you, but God will also place others in your life at strategic moments to encourage, stimulate, and challenge you to fulfill God's purpose for your life. These relationships are what put us on the right path.

There is a spiritual force that draws us and binds us to those who are a part of our destiny. We call that the "witness of the spirit." You will meet people on your journey who are obviously a part of God's plan for your life. Without these special friends, life is greatly diminished. Applying the wisdom of Solomon, let us take a look at the contributions friends make in our lives.

Laboring Together

Any task is easier when someone is along to help. It was this concept that inspired Solomon to write, "Two are better than one" (Eccles. 4:9). Jesus knew this principle. He sent forth His disciples two-by-two so they would encourage each other and hold each other accountable. Two people can accomplish more together. God designed it that way. Michael Jordan needed Scottie Pippen to win six NBA titles with the Chicago Bulls in the nineties. Kobe Bryant needed Shaquille O'Neal to experience their dominance during the first decade of the new millennium. LeBron James needed Dwyane Wade to win his first NBA championship in 2012. Muhammad Ali needed Joe Frazier to push him to be the greatest boxer in the history of the world. They would become great friends. Magic Johnson and Larry Bird had a similar relationship—a friendship that challenged them to work harder.

Friendship ought to take you higher and move you into

your destiny. Billy Graham needed George Beverly Shea to go into the world and preach the gospel message of Jesus Christ. In the early days Shea turned down many lucrative offers to travel with this young evangelist.[1] The story of Billy Graham and George Beverly Shea is one of true friendship that put them both on the path God had planned for them and that sent them around the world with the gospel.

Do you have people in your life who inspire you, challenge you, love you, and are willing to lay down their own ambitions for a greater cause? If not, you need to ask yourself if you have soul mates, teammates, or cell mates.

SOUL MATES, TEAMMATES, OR CELL MATES?

Are your relationships rewarding? Ecclesiastes 4:9 says, "They have a good return for their work" (NIV). Who wants to achieve or win with no one nearby to witness it? When you hit the ball over the fence, win an award, get that raise, or complete a project, you want those you love to share your joy.

I serve as the vice president of a local youth association here in Chattanooga, Tennessee. I have coached Little League baseball, football, and basketball for kids ages five to twelve for the last seven years, and I have learned much about this generation and its problems. Many of these kids are being raised by single moms, single dads, or one or more of their grandparents. I have stepped into the father's role for some of the kids who have played for me. It goes far beyond coaching for me. Sometimes I have had to rebuke parents for setting a bad example for their kids. Sometimes I have had to raise money or spend my own money to help families.

I coached one boy whose dad was addicted to prescription drugs and was in and out of his life for the five years I coached this boy. The boy was one of the best leaders who ever played for me, but in pressure situations he would get very tense and lose his confidence because of his father's actions. His father would either be in jail or high in the stands acting inappropriately. All this young man ever wanted was for his dad to be there and share in his accomplishments. I have seen children hit the game-winning home run or make a game-saving tackle and not have Mommy or Daddy there to see it. That is why kids join gangs and secret societies.

Kids need to know they are loved and feel like they are a part of something that matters. Churches need to adopt this approach in their children's ministries. They need to start fathering and mothering the next generation, not coddling middle- and upper-class parents who want their kids to be the focal point of the stage for every play, performance, or Little League game.

Early in my ministry the Lord called me to serve as senior pastor of an inner-city church in Atlanta for a year. This was great training ground for me. After being there for a month or so, I learned that the inner-city kids had a separate youth program from the more affluent students from the faithful core of the church. I shared with the leadership that this was something I would most definitely and immediately change. How can we show the love of Christ to a lost and dying world when we try to segregate ourselves from the rest of the world?

Here in Chattanooga many of the middle-class families are sending their kids to Christian schools. Churches are starting schools every other year. I don't know how we are preparing our kids for what they will face in college or in the real world by trying to shelter them from the real world. I think Christian schools are great, but the Bible tells us to be in the world, but not of the world (John 17:13–16).

No matter how old we get, when something good comes to us, whether it is honor, opportunity, or reward, we know that there were other people who helped lift us to that place. Could it be that your soul mate or teammate might be a different color than you? Could it be that your soul mate or teammate might be from a different nation than you? Could it be that your soul mate or teammate might be a different gender than you? Could it be that your soul mate or teammate might have been raised poor or maybe even in extreme wealth? I want to encourage you not to segregate yourself but to be open to different cultures, different people, and new ideas.

We've talked about soul mates and teammates and how important they are, but now let's talk about cell mates. I saw a quote on Facebook the other day that said something like, "A good friend will come and bail you out of jail, but a true friend will be sitting right beside you saying, 'Man, that was fun.'" It is a sad day we live in when that is the contemporary definition of a good friend. Friendships are supposed to pick you up when you fall. Ecclesiastes 4:10 says, "If one falls down, his friend can help him up. But pity the man who falls and has no one to help him up!" (NIV).

A cell mate is the opposite of a teammate and a soul mate. A cell mate is someone who is in prison with you and would rather you stay in prison with him than gain your freedom. These types of people do not want to see you break free and live an extraordinary, blessed, and favored life. Your prison may be sin, defeat, disappointment, addiction, lack of education, financial debt, or just failure in general. Misery loves company. A cell mate is a codependent person who is your friend as long as you are in prison with him. They will tell stories, make jokes, and share favors with you as long as you are living a mediocre and miserable life with them. But when you start trying to gain your freedom from your past and move into a place of blessing, they will resent you for it. They will be jealous and resentful. Some cell mates will even make attempts to destroy your accomplishments or make light of them. You need friends who will help you recover from failure, who will pick you up, and who long to see you prosper and do well.

Every year thousands of young athletes from all over the world gather for the Special Olympics. The fanfare, celebrities, music, and excitement are nearly as grand as the regular Olympics. These athletes know what it means to give their best. They have trained for months and for years and want to win. The following story was retold in *Stories for the Heart*:

> Several years ago, five handicapped finalists gathered at the starting line. Their hearts were pounding. Each wanted to win. The starter's gun discharged and the athletes exploded from their crouched positions and began running with all their heart. The crowd was on its feet shouting and cheering. Suddenly one of the runners stumbled and fell flat on his face. He struggled but couldn't seem to get up. A moan and then a hush fell over the stadium. In the next moment, another child stopped running and reached down and helped the fallen child back up. Holding hands, the two runners finished the race together.[2]
> —MICHAEL BROOME

Also, if two lie down together, they will keep warm. But
how can one keep warm alone?
—Ecclesiastes 4:11, niv

Here are some of the supernatural blessings that come
upon your life when you are connected with genuine soul
mates and teammates.

Genuine Agreement Guarantees Victory Over the Enemy

Though one may be overpowered, two can defend themselves. A cord of three strands is not quickly broken.
—Ecclesiastes 4:12, niv

In spiritual warfare, two can fight better than one. Jesus
reminded His disciples, "Again, I tell you that if two of you on
earth agree about anything you ask for, it will be done for you
by my Father in heaven. For where two or three come together
in my name, there am I with them" (Matt. 18:19–20, niv).

You see, there is a mystery in friendship and partnership
that brings on the third strand of the rope—the Lord! When
two bind their hearts together, the Lord is bound to them to
answer their prayers. In a powerful way, He links Himself
with them in power and authority. This is another reason
Jesus sent the disciples out two-by-two. He knew that friendship was going to be one of the secrets of power and victory in their lives. He placed them in relationships with other
people, and in doing so unleashed His power in every facet
and in every season of their lives.

GENUINE AGREEMENT RELEASES ANSWERS TO PRAYER

As we read above, Matthew 18:19–20 promises that prayers are answered when two people agree. We don't have friendship so that we can just grin at each other! Moments come in your life when a person says to you, "I have a burden. I have a need." You agree to pray about the need, believing that God is going to break through in their lives. Or perhaps in a time of need you had been in a prayer meeting with a friend, when all of a sudden you were transported by God's grace out of that place of fear. In an instant, what was worrying you doesn't worry you anymore. That is the power of a friend's prayer.

GENUINE AGREEMENT INVOKES THE PRESENCE OF GOD

Not only does friendship release the power of prayer, but it also brings on the very presence of Jesus. Matthew wrote that Christ said, "There am I with them" (Matt. 18:20, NIV). That is the threefold cord of the New Testament. You may say, "Well, He is with me when I am alone." Yes, but sometimes you need someone else nearby to remind you that He is there.

When Dad was a younger man, he could live in solitude. Just ask Mom. He could go off for a weeklong revival speaking engagement and not care if anybody spoke to him or spent time with him! But the older Dad's become, the more he knows he cannot do the task of the ministry alone. There needs to be partners who are praying. There must be people who are standing with you.

Genuine Agreement Fortifies You When You Are Under Attack

Genuine friendships and alliances are the secret of power over the darkness. Mark 6:7 states, "He sent them out two by two and gave them authority over unclean spirits" (NIV). The Lord chose to use teams of at least two, promising His own gracious presence. This is especially needful when facing the attacks of Satan and his demonic forces. A strong piece of advice: don't ever do spiritual warfare alone. He sent them forth two-by-two, and He became the third One on every team.

Genuine Agreement Strengthens Faith in Times of Hopelessness

You may recall the story of the two disciples on the Emmaus road, as Luke recounted in chapter 24 of his gospel. The two men were walking up the road, and as the Greek language puts it, "they were hurling words against each other" as they talked of Jesus's death and the rumor that He had risen from the dead. They were walking along in unbelief, still feeling that Jesus was in the grave. These men had not embraced the resurrection. They were in unbelief but were sincere in seeking after the truth. Then gloriously, the Truth showed up right beside them!

They finally arrived at their house and invited Jesus to stay. No doubt it was as He broke the bread after sharing the Word that they must have seen the scars in His hands and they exclaimed, "Jesus!" But look at verses 32–33 (NIV):

185

"Were not our hearts burning within us when he talked
to us on the road and opened the Scriptures to us?"
They got up at once and returned to Jerusalem.

These two friends had their hearts set ablaze by Jesus Christ. It is possible for two people to share the same burning passion for Jesus and partner to tell others the story.

There is a moving story of a minister faced with tragedy. Wes Anderson, pastor of Carmichael Christian Church in Sacramento, California, was feeling blessed to be involved in such a wonderful ministry. One day, he saw one of his elderly members stopped on the roadside with her car broken down. He stopped to assist her. Suddenly a speeding car came upon them and crushed the pastor against the stranded vehicle. He nearly died as a result of his injuries and tragically lost his leg. Being single, he faced this crisis only with the support of his church.

When a newspaper carried his heroic story, the article caught the attention of a young single mom. She found her faith lifted by his courage and decided on a whim to visit him. It was a meeting of destiny. Across the months of his recovery, she became his best friend.

One day on an outing with the single mom, the pastor took a serious fall. He was frustrated and embarrassed at his plight, but she calmly and easily came to his aid and helped him up. This gentle act made him realize how much he loved her and that he did not want to live alone. These two friends fell in love and are now happily married.[3]

This young single mom took a chance by embracing the possibility that God might have a soul mate out there for her. Her soul mate is now her teammate, and they are a shining example of a cord of three strands that is not easily broken. They now travel the world sharing the gospel and working as a team.

Get rid of the cell mates and embrace the soul mates and teammates that God has for you.

A Unique Friendship

Most men find it very difficult to be close with other men. With the rise of homosexuality, men hesitate to express their feelings to each other due to fear of what others may think. Men are afraid to weep publicly, embrace one another, or share their feelings on an emotional level because they are afraid someone might call them gay.

Some of my closest friends are my male friends who believe in me and with whom I can share my dreams. Men are starved for real friendship. My challenge to the men across the world is that we get in agreement with each other and "man up." We need to build relationships with other men! I believe this camaraderie and support from one another will reform our culture, restore our families, and rewrite our destiny.

Many truths can be found in the story of Jonathan and David in the Bible. See David's words about Jonathan after his death:

> I grieve [am distressed] for you, Jonathan my brother;
> you were very dear to me. Your love for me was won-
> derful, more wonderful than that of women.
> —2 Samuel 1:26, niv

A word study reveals much about this verse. The word *distressed* means "to suffer cramps in the abdomen." David was hurting over his "brother." The word *brother* means one who is "like me, who resembles me, who has an affinity with me." In describing the relationship as "wonderful," David elevates it to "miraculous" as he uses the Hebrew *pele*. The word *love* here in the Hebrew, *ahav*, is equivalent to the New Testament word *agape*.

What is the significance of all those Hebrew words? Just this: David viewed his friendship with Jonathan as a delightful, wonderful miracle. When you view their friendship, you are seeing the greatest known friendship in all of the Old Testament. Friendship at its best is the highest and most lasting of all relationships.

As we look at this relationship, it mirrors for us the kind of genuine connection we need to have in our lives.

Soul to soul

There must be a soul-to-soul relationship. In 1 Samuel 18:1 we read, "the soul of Jonathan was knit with the soul of David" (KJV). The word "soul" translated as *nephesh*, which means one's life force. It is the word used in Genesis 2:7, "And the LORD God...breathed into his nostrils the breath of life; and man became a living soul" (KJV). In that moment their very beings were tied together. The best of friendship ties the lives and destinies of people together.

Self-giving love

Self-sacrificing love is always present if friendship is to flourish. Just think about the implications of 1 Samuel 18:1, "Jonathan loved him as his own soul" (KJV). This love was a self-giving spirit as well as a deep affection for one's friend. Jonathan was content to simply be David's friend.

Henry David Thoreau said, "The most I can do for my friend is simply to be his friend. I have no wealth to bestow on him. If he knows that I am happy in loving him, he will want no reward. Is not friendship divine in this?"[4]

Jonathan asked nothing of David but rather surrendered all that he had to his friend. Jonathan never asked David for more than a deep friendship.

Surrender of ambitions

The deeper level of friendship leads you to surrender your own ambition to assist your friend. Notice in 1 Samuel 18:3–4, Jonathan makes a covenant with David and surrenders his robe and armor to him. In this act, Jonathan recognizes the special calling of David and surrenders his own right to the throne. Thus the uncrowned king becomes an ally and protector of David.

Those who would be friends to those anointed for leadership must surrender their own ambitions for the vision of the leader. Those with their own agenda can never be close to their leader. The greatest example of this may very well be Elisha. Elisha killed his oxen, burned his plows, and followed Elijah faithfully until the end. His steadfastness and devotion are the model for all those who would be friends of their leaders.

Survives circumstances

Friendship will transcend all circumstances. In 1 Samuel 20:4, we discover the depths of Jonathan's loyalty to David. This loyalty knows no bounds. Listen to Jonathan: "Whatever you want me to do, I'll do it for you" (NIV). This verse reveals to us the tender scene of separation when their tears mingle, and they promise to love each other and their respective descendants forever.

Real friends can weep together. In your time of crisis, you

may discover that your greatest need is to have someone just be there not saying a thing. In grief, the adage is true, "The less said, the better."

Years ago I had a dear pastor friend who wronged his family in an intense personal failure. He called me in grief and remorse, admitting that he was as a dead man with nothing to live for. Days later he suffered a massive heart attack. As I sat by his hospital bed, we cried together word-lessly. This grief was not something that could be discussed away; it could not be contained in words. Those shared tears were the only comfort I could offer my friend in his last days.

It is significant to note that when told of Lazarus's death, Jesus simply wept. He did not feel it necessary to explain the doctrine of death. In a time of crisis, He knew the value of tears. No doubt He remembered the scripture that tells how precious tears are to the Father: "You number my wan-derings; put my tears into Your bottle; are they not in Your book?" (Ps. 56:8).

Reaching beyond the grave

Death does not end real friendship. In 1 Samuel 20:42 Jonathan makes a pledge of friendship that will last for generations:

> Jonathan said to David, "Go in peace, for we have sworn friendship with each other in the name of the LORD, saying, 'The LORD is witness between you and me, and between your descendants and my descendants forever.'"
>
> —NIV

After Jonathan's death, David brought Jonathan's son, Mephibosheth, to his own table. This story is a thrilling one.

A nurse had dropped Mephibosheth as a baby, and as a result, both of his legs were crippled. After his grandfather, Saul, and his father, Jonathan, were killed in battle, he fell into poverty until David remembered his promise to Jonathan and sent his servant after the young man. In light of the poverty, pain, and destitution that Jonathan's son had come to know, it is interesting that he lived at a barren place aptly named Lodebar, or "no pasture." The name *Lodebar* means the "dry place." The name *Mephibosheth* means "shame unto you."

Guilt and shame will cause most of us to isolate ourselves and settle into an empty and dry place. Mephibosheth was carried to the land of Gilead, where he found refuge in the house of Machir, son of Ammiel, by whom he was reared. The name *Machir* has a hidden meaning. It means "slavery." Shame will often lead us to the dry place and then into slavery. There is another controversial figure in this story named Ziba. The name *Ziba* means "no progress."

If you aren't making any progress in life, it might just be that you are on the wrong path, in the wrong place, and around the wrong people. Guilt will lead you into isolation (Lodebar). Isolation will cause you to become a slave (Machir) to your past and shame. Slavery, guilt, and isolation will cause you to be stuck, unable to move forward with your life (Ziba).

Yet in the face of that broken young man, David (his name meaning "salvation or redemption") saw his dearest friend, Jonathan. Mephibosheth was brought to the palace, where his crippled feet were placed under the king's table! He was reared as David's own son! What a poignant reminder of the fact that being in the company of a genuine friend brings you to a large and prosperous place and that no matter what your past was, you can still live a life under the blessing of God.

THE ETERNAL COVENANT OF
GENUINE AGREEMENT

It was May 5, 2001. I had been married just a few months, and my wife and I were expecting our first child. I was almost twenty, and my life had taken a sudden change. Instead of partying with my friends and attending school, I found myself at an entry level corporate job trying to buy furniture for our first small home. I had recently cut ties with some of my best friends from my upbringing. I had no choice, as many of them were still living as teenagers, and I had forfeited my right to be a kid. I was a husband and about to be a father, and I desperately wanted to be a good one.

I got a call one morning from my former youth pastor.

"Ronnie, this is Brian. Do you remember Derek Simmons?"

"Yes," I answered, "he is one of my best friends, but I haven't talked to him in a couple of months."

"I have some bad news. He died this morning."

I jumped up out of bed and said, "What?"

"I am at the hospital, and he was just pronounced dead," he said.

I burst into tears and hung up the phone.

Derek and I had been friends since we were eleven years old. We grew up playing basketball and football together. We had spent countless times at each other's houses. His parents and grandparents were members of Abba's House. Derek was a blond-haired, blue-eyed boy with a personality that drew people toward him. He and I both were mischievous as kids and loved to laugh. We had both lost our grandfathers at the same age and had a lot in common.

In high school we were both pretty popular. We attended

parties and dabbled in alcohol and drugs. We went on double dates together and were around each other nearly every weekend. Most of our friends were the same.

After I graduated and went to college, Derek had one more year of high school to go. Derek, being the young entrepreneur that he was, realized that he could furnish himself and his friends with an abundance of marijuana if he sold it on the side. So he built relationships with people from some rough areas and started to sell marijuana on a small scale to his friends. The relationships he formed proved to be very destructive well after high school. These relationships opened the door to new designer drugs such as ecstasy, LSD, cocaine, and prescription drugs. Many of us experimented with these things, because we were with people we trusted and the drugs were inexpensive due to Derek's venture with selling marijuana.

Derek continued down this path for a couple of years after high school, and his drug use became more intense. I was with him for the first year of this progression but not for the end of it.

The last time I remember speaking with Derek was about a year prior to his death. We were both very upset and convicted for the life we had been living. I told Derek I felt God had called me to ministry. He agreed and encouraged me to do it. He said he felt I would do great things for the Lord. He then told me he was eventually going to stop living like he was and that it was just a phase.

He longed to be a fireman like his father and take over his father's construction business. He was a great Sheetrock man, and I know he would have done well expanding the business.

At the time of our last phone conversation Derek's circle of friends was changing, with the exception of a few people he kept in contact with from his early years. Many of his friends from adolescence had grown out of the experimental phase. Not to say they were walking with the Lord, but they were not as entangled in that lifestyle as he had become.

After I hung up the phone with my former student pastor, I jumped in my vehicle and drove as fast as I could to the Simmons's home, where I had practically grown up. I was crying so much that I could barely see the road. I was hoping somehow that if I got there soon enough Derek would be alive. I pulled up the long driveway through the woods to Derek's house. People were everywhere in the driveway, and I could hear a wailing, moaning scream like I have heard only one other time in my life. It was the cry of a distraught mother in her bedroom.

I immediately ran to Derek's father, and he asked me if I had been with Derek the night before. I told him that I hadn't spoken with him in five months because I was trying to get my life in order for the baby. Then I grabbed his brother, Colt, who was extremely upset. I spent that day with Derek's dad, uncle, and brother trying to piece together whom he had been with, where he had gone, and what exactly happened the night before.

His parents had received a knock at the door around five that morning. The person told them that Derek's girlfriend's car was found wrecked at the bottom of their long driveway. This was strange, as a week before his truck had rolled down this long driveway in neutral and hit the same tree where this car was wrecked on May 5, 2001. They found Derek unresponsive beside the car. The story they were told did not add up.

Derek had purchased some pills that he had never taken before just two days prior to his death. A lady in her forties had sold the prescription drug Oxycontin to Derek so she could replace a part on her car. Derek had never taken these particular drugs before. This drug is considered a street drug now, but it wasn't in 2001. This drug is like heroin, people say. Derek took one and a half of the pills and mixed them with a little alcohol and marijuana around ten the night before. His parents and I believe that he died around people who didn't care enough about him to call an ambulance or protect him. We believe he died in his sleep at a friend's house. We believe his accident was staged at the bottom of his parents' long driveway to make it appear that he died in an accident at home.

This was a terrible way for a young man to die, but the drugs had caused his relationships to change. He ended up spending his last night on earth with people who couldn't care less about him. He was isolated, making no progress, surrounded by the wrong kinds of people.

Derek had accepted Christ at a young age and had lived for the Lord at one time. He was touched as a young teen in one of our services and lived that roller-coaster lifestyle that many teens do.

His death was a tragedy, and the guilt consumed me. Why Derek? Why now? Why didn't they call 911? What if I would have called him or witnessed to him?

After a year or so our church performed a play about his death dedicated to his memory. I spoke each night at the end of the play and gave the altar call. Over two thousand people accepted Christ, and fifteen hundred students made a commitment to abstain from abusing drugs. It didn't fill the void of him being gone, but God used it in a Romans 8:28 kind of way.

His parents struggled with every aspect of life for the next eight years. His mother's emotional and physical health deteriorated, and his father battled guilt, anger, and depression. I stayed in touch with them and in relationship with them over the years. I called them when I came back to the Lord and would invite them to come hear me preach from time to time. They eventually would come and see what God was doing in my life. We took them on vacation with us to Destin, Florida, in 2010. They initially didn't want to go, but they did, and we had a wonderful time. His mother, Susie, felt like the Lord began to heal her from lupus on this trip. I believe God used this trip to heal a number of hurts in their lives.

Fast-forward to the present. They are both serving our community. His dad, Clay, is now a deacon in our church, and Derek's little brother is on the verge of starting his family. They are our extended family. "Why?" you might ask. Because Derek and I had a covenant relationship that lasted after he passed away. His family loves me because he loved me. I love them because he loved them. My friendship with Derek transcended a decade.

I have seen more than seven thousand people accept Christ when I have told his story in crusades, revivals, schools, and rehabs. His parents have encouraged me to keep telling the story. His parents are serving God in a deeper way than they ever have. My three boys love to stay with them and spend time with them. All of my boys know who Derek was. Derek's father, Clay, coaches Little League baseball with me for kids ages five to twelve and gives back to the boys and girls of our community.

Sometimes relationships do last beyond the grave. Sometimes a covenant from years past can still transform lives years later. Like Jesus's. His covenant from more than two thousand years ago is still changing lives today around the world.

Chapter 15

AGREEMENT IN THE FAMILY OF GOD

By Ronnie Phillips Jr.

This chapter is dedicated to the loving and faithful members of Abba's House, who have loved and supported our family through the years.

M Y ENTIRE LIFE has been spent in the local church. I have seen the good, the bad, and the ugly. I have seen how hurtful the church can be, but I have also seen how loving a church can be. It truly is the body of Christ. My wife and I have developed some lifelong friendships because we were joined and jointed to God's kingdom through His body. I met my wife in church. I got saved, filled with the Holy Spirit, and baptized in a local church. The most meaningful times in one's life ought to be in God's house. For many churches today, a major factor missing is the ability to build quality relationships with one another in the church.

In our megachurches we have decided to entertain the

masses instead of impacting the culture. In our smaller churches we have decided to stick to our own race, rules, and way of thinking instead of reaching the lost and impacting our community. Mega or mini is not the issue at hand. The issue at hand is one of mind-set.

Churches struggle with a number of issues such as legalism, which is why they are more concerned with upholding rules than operating in grace. Secular humanism is another disease that plagues the church. This is when the church tries to conform to the culture and fit in with the world. Traditionalism is doing things out of a need to keep the status quo rather than allowing the Holy Spirit to manage our gatherings. Mysticism is something I see in some of our more charismatic churches. People are so hungry for the Lord that they will operate in the flesh and act out rather than waiting on God for the true power of the Holy Spirit to come upon them.

We recently returned from the Dominican Republic, where there was a strong voodoo spirit in one of our crusades. People spun around and around rapidly until they passed out during worship. They were so desperate for a genuine touch that they would try anything.

Ritualism is another issue many churches are struggling with in the day in which we live. Ritualism is doing things the same way you have always done them instead of trying new things.

We recently had our people take Communion as a family in one of our main services. We had them walk down the aisle as a family instead of passing the traditional trays. We kept the biblical precedent, but it was so powerful to allow the Holy Spirit to lead us in a different direction. We had worship in between the bread and the wine, and the Holy Spirit was moving mightily.

The last thing that plagues our churches and specifically our relationships with other Christians is denominationalism. It is very sad to me the way that most evangelical denominations judge the charismatic denominations, and how the charismatics judge the evangelicals. I was raised Southern Baptist, and I remember the controversy our church faced when we started worshipping differently during our services and praying for the sick.

The truth is, we are all on the same team. We are both evangelical and charismatic. The connection between these two streams could have a major impact on the kingdom if we ever came together. That is a dream my father and I pray will one day become a reality.

What counters the attack of the enemy in the local church? What makes life in the church worth doing? I believe it is as simple as finding agreement in the things that really matter and building quality relationships.

RESIST THE RELIGIOUS SPIRIT

Nothing on earth is more wonderful than a true friend; however, there is also nothing more disappointing than a false friend. Job had endured every onslaught of hell and survived; Satan had been resisted and had fled! But then his friends came for a visit, and in reading the account, one comes to the conclusion that Job fared better against the devil than he did in the hands of his friends!

Listen to Job's heart in Job 19:13–21 (NIV):

He has alienated my brothers from me; my acquaintances are completely estranged from me. My kinsmen have gone away; my friends have forgotten me. My guests and my maidservants count me as a stranger; they look upon me as an alien. I summon my servant, but he does not answer, though I beg him with my own mouth. My breath is offensive to my wife; I am loathsome to my own brothers. Even the little boys scorn me; when I appear, they ridicule me. All my intimate friends detest me; those I love have turned against me. I am nothing but skin and bones; I have escaped with only the skin of my teeth. Have pity on me, my friends, have pity, for the hand of God has struck me.

Job's three friends Eliphaz, Bildad, and Zophar let him down in his moment of most desperate need. Of course, these men are to be commended for caring enough to visit in the first place. Their motive was right, but their method was wrong. They ventured beyond their place as comforters to become critics. They took up where the devil had left off!

Notice their words of "comfort." Eliphaz declares to Job, "You have sinned," and, "You are being chastened" (Job 4:7–8; 5:17–18). Bildad says, "You need to repent," and Zophar is blunt: "You deserve more punishment" (Job 8:1–6)

Throughout the rest of their sage advice, we find other such gems such as:

"You are a windbag."

"You are empty-headed."

"You need to shut up."

"You do not know God."

"You are a maggot and a worm." (See Job 8–25.)

The old adage "With friends like these, who needs enemies" comes to mind as we think of Job sitting in his misery!

What was the problem with these friends? Forget for a moment about Job's condition. The fact is, the friends do not agree. They fight over an issue and they argue. Soon insults are hurled back and forth. These friendships were destroyed because they were unwilling to be wrong. Lies were spoken against Job. When you read the context, Job has become the victim of the religious, legalistic tongues of others. His life is a byword to the nation for sin.

Hear Job's appraisal of their friendship:

"You mock me."

"You are worthless physicians."

"You are miserable comforters."

"You torment my soul." (See Job 12–13; 16; and 19.)

Notice that all three friends were religious types. They all cited God as the Source of their wisdom as they tore Job apart at the seams. Religious people can be among the most brutal individuals in the world. You must be careful even at church to (1) not be this person and (2) stay clear of people who are like this. It's contagious.

DON'T BE SUPER SPIRITUAL

In Job 4 and 5 Eliphaz promises Job health and wealth if he will just repent. This false friend goes on to remind Job of what he used to be:

> Then Eliphaz the Temanite replied: "If someone ventures a word with you, will you be impatient? But who can keep from speaking? Think how you have instructed many, how you have strengthened feeble hands. Your

words supported those who stumbled; you have strengthened faltering knees. But now trouble comes to you, and you are discouraged; it strikes you, and you are dismayed. Should not your piety be your confidence and your blameless ways your hope?"

—JOB 4:1–6, NIV

"Job," says this religious friend, "you used to be somebody in the church!" In the following verses, he blasts Job, claiming that Job was the cause of his own problems. Then comes the knock-out punch for Eliphaz. He claims to have had a vision and word of knowledge from God about Job:

A word was secretly brought to me, my ears caught a whisper of it. Amid disquieting dreams in the night, when deep sleep falls on men, fear and trembling seized me and made all my bones shake. A spirit glided past my face, and the hair on my body stood on end. It stopped, but I could not tell what it was. A form stood before my eyes, and I heard a hushed voice: "Can a mortal be more righteous than God? Can a man be more pure than his Maker? If God places no trust in his servants, if he charges his angels with error, how much more those who live in houses of clay, whose foundations are in the dust, who are crushed more readily than a moth! Between dawn and dusk they are broken to pieces; unnoticed, they perish forever. Are not the cords of their tent pulled up, so that they die without wisdom?"

—JOB 4:12–21, NIV

This supposed experience with God was concerning Job. You may be wondering, "Why would God not speak this word to Job Himself?" Christian emotion, experience, and ecstasy can happen, and there is nothing wrong with those things.

Yet from the context, it appears that here Eliphaz had trafficked with a demon, not the Holy Spirit, for the message was a false one. We find that later God Himself confronted Eliphaz:

> And it was so, that after the LORD had spoken these words unto Job, the LORD said to Eliphaz the Temanite, My wrath is kindled against thee, and against thy two friends: for ye have not spoken of me the thing that is right, as my servant Job hath. Therefore...go to my servant Job, and offer up for yourselves a burnt offering; and my servant Job shall pray for you...lest I deal with you after your folly.
>
> —JOB 42:7–8, KJV

Eliphaz had not spoken in wisdom. As a true member in the body of Christ, you will allow the Holy Spirit to shape your words with God's truth before you deliver them to a brother or sister. Save the super-spiritual dramatics and seek a genuine connection with God so that He will reveal to you the right way to approach your colaborers.

Primarily, God gives His word to us through the Bible. Scripture must confirm any revelation that occurs outside of Scripture. The enemy will often try to send messages from people (and even through you) who seem to be mystical or even spiritual. Watch out for those who are always claiming special revelations.

GUARD AGAINST JUDGMENTALISM

"Ah, Job!" said Bildad, "If you are pure and upright, even now he will rouse himself on your behalf and restore you to your rightful place" (Job 8:6, NIV). His accusation was that Job had not lived a separated life! In verse 8 he continues, "Ask the former generations." What Job needed to do, according to this friend, was to get back to the great teaching of the past.

There is absolutely nothing wrong with fundamental theology. There is much wrong with a legalistic, judgmental attitude toward others, especially toward the suffering. The legalist values rules more than relationships. Often this person has his faith in forms and outward Christianity.

SAVE YOUR KNOW-IT-ALLS

These are the people who quote verses out of context all the time.

> You say to God, "My beliefs are flawless and I am pure in your sight." Oh, how I wish that God would speak, that he would open his lips against you and disclose to you the secrets of wisdom.
>
> —JOB 11:4–6, NIV

Here, Zophar accuses Job of being a fundamentalist and promises him special wisdom. What Job needed, according to this friend, was a new wisdom or a new truth.

Today this trend is observed in those who want to give their latest best seller to the hurting. However, when you are hurting, the first thing you need is not a new book, but loving friends who will weep and pray with you. All the glib answers and religious clichés do little for a broken heart. At a later time in your healing, appropriate materials may be helpful to support you, but at the beginning of your pain, you need to hear a friend say, "I care." It is much easier to receive instruction in the context of a caring atmosphere. Remember this as you interact with members in your church community.

THE KIND OF PEOPLE THE BODY OF CHRIST NEEDS

Here are characteristics of people who truly advance the kingdom vision for the body of Christ:

They heal, not hurt.

Job had cried out for pity from his friends. He needed healers to come with compassion. Instead, he received criticism, verbal assault, and bad advice.

They comfort, not torment.

In Job 19:2, we hear Job's cry, "How long will [you] vex my soul, and break me in pieces with words?" (KJV). Friends need words of comfort, not biting criticism, when they are in pain.

They bring strength, not sarcasm.

Job knew what kind of friend he should have. This was his idea of a true friend:

> I also could speak like you do, if you were in my place; I could make fine speeches against you and shake my head at you. But my mouth would encourage you; comfort from my lips would bring you relief.
> —JOB 16:4–5, NIV

They are faithful to their suffering companions.

The church is often guilty of forgetting those who are suffering. The divorcée is forgotten by her married friends. The widower is neglected by couples who used to fellowship with him. True friendship remembers the better days and embraces the old friend who may be suffering. "A friend loves at all times," says Proverbs 17:1 (NIV).

The proper office of a friend is to side with you when you are in the wrong. Nearly anybody will side with you when you are in the right.[1]

—Mark Twain

Discover Your Redeemer Anew

So what was the outcome for Job? Well, of course, we read that God restored his possessions and family many times over. But the loss of his human friendships led to the greatest confession of faith in the Old Testament: "I know that my Redeemer lives..." (Job 19:25, NIV). Job had a Friend in heaven. That Redeemer came to earth and lived His own words, "Greater love has no one than this, that he lay down his life for his friends. You are my friends" (John 15:13–14, NIV).

Jesus loves us and longs for us to operate in love in the church. For the New Testament church, fellowship is outflow of the love of the indwelling Christ. We ought to love one another in the church because He first loved us. The church must be a place where people grow, learn, love, and work in unity as a body. It is a synergy that moves us into our divine purpose. There is a passage in Ephesians that sets forth the importance of agreement in the church as a necessity for growth:

> As a prisoner of the Lord, then, I urge you to live a life worthy of the calling you have received. Be completely humble and gentle; be patient, bearing with one another in love. Make every effort to keep the unity of the Spirit through the bond of peace. There is one body and one Spirit—just as you were called to one hope when you were called—one Lord, one faith, one baptism; one God and Father of all, who is over all and through all and

in all. But to each one of us grace has been given as Christ apportioned it. That is why it says: "When He ascended on high, he led captives in his train and gave gifts to men." (What does "he ascended" mean except that He also descended to the lower, earthly regions? He who descended is the very one who ascended higher than all the heavens, in order to fill the whole universe.) It was he who gave some to be apostles, some to be prophets, some to be evangelists, and some to be pastors and teachers, to prepare God's people for works of service, so that the body of Christ may be built up until we all reach unity in the faith and in the knowledge of the Son of God and become mature, attaining to the whole measure of the fullness of Christ. Then we will no longer be infants, tossed back and forth by the waves, and blown here and there by every wind of teaching and by the cunning and craftiness of men in their deceitful scheming. Instead, speaking the truth in love, we will in all things grow up into him who is the Head, that is, Christ. From him the whole body, joined and held together by every supporting ligament, grows and builds itself up in love, as each part does its work.

—EPHESIANS 4:1–16, NIV

The passage above contains an order to solid growth in a church that presents itself in a simple, easy-to-remember outline: divine glue—unity (Eph. 4:1–6), divine gifts—equipment (Eph. 4:7–11), and divine growth—inevitable (Eph. 4:12–13).

Divine glue—unity

For years we have tried to exercise gifts and experience growth without teaching the importance of unity. Unity is only possible in the atmosphere of true friendship.

Now there is a twofold unity mentioned in this passage:

the unity of the Spirit (4:3), and the unity of the faith (4:13). In the church we find these foundations of true friendship. They are in the proper order. Unity begins with the work of the Holy Spirit and moves to a unity of doctrine.

More often than not we try to teach people what to believe and what to do before we teach them who they are! In doing so, they come to the false understanding that church is something you believe or something you do.

Divine gifts—equipment

The first issue in church life ought to be the discovery and celebration of the uniqueness and giftedness of the individual member. Of course, churches should plan fellowship events for various groups to facilitate the formation of quality friendships. But a deeper step would be to establish a program like Networks, birthed by Willow Creek Community Church in Chicago, to help people to discover their own individual spiritual gifting and thus find their unique place in the church. Once that place is found, people tend to develop deep friendships with those around them who share like interests and gifting. Sound doctrine and faithful service must follow in that order. The unity of the Spirit should precede the unity of doctrine.

Divine growth—inevitable

Those in evangelical life may wonder why so many works are growing so rapidly among those out on the cutting edge of spiritual life. Evangelicals have solid methods and growth principles, yet the movement is outstripped often by those we classify as charismatics. Their secret is the unity of the Spirit first!

When Jesus spoke with the woman at the well, He advised

her, "They that worship him must worship him in spirit and in truth" (John 4:24, KJV). That is always the divine order.

You see, the divine presence is within you! A witness of the Spirit exists between believers. This witness of the Spirit is intangible but real. There is a spiritual spark and attraction between you and other people who share divine destiny! When you surround yourself in the church with friends with whom you share the Spirit and truth, then growth is inevitable. This growth includes the "growing up" of maturity as well as the numerical growth of ministry.

A church ought to be full of people who have found fulfilling connections with others. Look at that phrase in Ephesians 4:16: "joined and held together by every supporting ligament" (NIV). How is it that we can be that close to others in the body of Christ? In Romans 12, another passage on spiritual giftedness, Paul sets forth our responsibilities to one another:

> Just as each of us has one body with many members,
> and these members do not all have the same function,
> so in Christ we who are many form one body, and each
> member belongs to all the others.
> —ROMANS 12:4–5, NIV

There are three important lessons you should know about dependence on others.

OUR SPIRITUAL VITALITY DEPENDS ON OUR DEPENDENCE ON ONE ANOTHER

The imagery of the physical body is used to describe the church. A body is made up of many members such as feet, hands, eyes, and ears. The gifts of the Spirit (see the *Gifts of Spirit* by Dr. Ron Phillips) characterize where each person fits as a member. Now, if you cut yourself off from the members of the body where God has set you, then you die.

Suppose my hand got mad at me. "I saw you clipping your toenails, but you didn't clip the fingernails. You've been spending more time on those toenails than the fingernails, so I am not going to function for you any longer!" So my right hand decides that it is going to quit working for me. It has a meeting with the left hand, saying, "Left hand, let me tell you something. Did you notice how carefully he clipped his toenails and how he has barely spent any time with us? I mean, he barely remembers to bite off the nails on me when they get too long; he just hasn't treated us right! That old big mouth; we just won't have anything to do with the mouth or the head anymore." So they both go on strike.

Well, somewhere along the line they meet the feet. Sitting in the bathtub one day, they happen upon one another. They say to the feet, "If I were you, I wouldn't take him anywhere anymore. Even though he has treated you better, the truth is that he treats his hair better than he does the rest of us." So then the feet decide not to carry me to the table, the hands are not going to feed me, and after two months of this, I finally die! Guess who died with me? The hands and the feet! If the body dies, they die. I need them, and they need me.

Somehow when it comes to church, we have trouble under-standing this concept! Churches tend to cluster around one gift and resist the riches of spiritual diversity. In a big church, each member cannot know everybody, just as there are some organs in my body that I will never touch. I doubt if I'll ever hold my liver in my hand; at least, I hope there is not much chance of that! I have no desire to touch it, but I am really glad it is functioning! In the life of the church, you will never be able to touch and influence every person, but in your circle or small group there are friendships to nurture. That small circle is a part of the whole and is a part of what God is doing.

Just as one day I realized I could not live without the friends surrounding me, I hope you realize that you cannot live without your friends in your spiritual life. How desperately we need each other. The *Good Life Almanac* says, "No man is the whole of himself. His friends are the rest of him."[2]

Somehow, when I came to know Jesus Christ and began to meet Christian friends, I began to find out the rest of who I am. I have discovered the joy of a life of agreement with others.

There may be those of you who are reading this and thinking, "I can have my spiritual life without a church." No, my friend, you need the church. It is essential to your spiritual health. Don't cut yourself off from your church just because you don't agree with everything going on. There are some things about your own body that you don't like and that you would like to straighten out. If that is true about the physical body, then it is certainly true of the church. You must continue being faithful to the Lord and let Him attend to the changes that need to be made. We are members of one another. Our spiritual life depends on it. Don't adopt a lone-ranger theology, where you cling to a prayer from when you were eight years old. You need people, and they need you. You need Jesus, and He wants you. The church is His body. It the place He has ordained for you to be connected to until His triumphant return.

OUR EMOTIONAL HEALTH DEPENDS ON OUR DEPENDENCE ON ONE ANOTHER

Be devoted to one another in brotherly love.
—ROMANS 12:10, NIV

One needs the affection and love of others. No doubt Robert Louis Stevenson had this in mind when he wrote, "So long as we are loved by others, I would almost say that we are indispensable: and no man is useless while he has a friend."[3]

THE BLESSING THAT COMES FROM HONOR DEPENDS ON OUR DEPENDENCE ON ONE ANOTHER

Honor one another above yourselves.
—ROMANS 12:10, NIV

Nothing thrills me more than to honor men and women of God who have gone before me and have traveled roads I have not yet traveled. If you want to be blessed, start honoring others even if you don't agree with them and watch how God promotes you. In the church we must not jockey for position and power. We must honor one another and raise up sons and daughters in the ministry.

At times we all must be the accompanist rather than the soloist. Sometimes the function of a pastor is to applaud others or to quietly make it possible for others to become all God wants them to be. We are to be encouragers. We must honor those people God has placed in the church with us.

Look around you when you come into the church. Do you see people without whom your life would be greatly diminished? If you really had a desperate need, to whom could you go and know that he would not fail to help you?

There are many people at Abba's House who have blessed my family and whom I could call no matter what. I would not be where I am today if it weren't for the people of Abba's House who have loved me my entire life.

The glue that holds a church together is our friendships with one another. Like marriage, true friendship can be "till death us do part."

A FEW CLOSING THOUGHTS ABOUT DIVISION AND STRIFE

Sometimes in the church there is division and strife. These things must be dealt with ruthlessly. We should confront people in accordance with Matthew 18 when they are causing havoc within the church. Our goal is to give people every chance to repent and be restored, but there are times when people must be removed from the body of Christ until they repent. This should always be the last resort.

People need to trust the leadership of their pastoral staff in dealing with these issues. Rest assured they know more of the story than the majority of the church body does, despite whatever rumors may have been spread about the person in question. Trust your leadership and always err on the side of grace.

This is our philosophy at Abba's House. Our goal is to restore people to fellowship within the body when they sin or cause division. We will exhaust all resources to show grace to the hurting, just as Christ did for us. He poured Himself out and exhausted all resources so that we may have life and have it more abundantly.

BOUNDARIES, NOT WALLS

I N THE WONDERFUL new book *Cross Roads* by William Paul Young (author of the best-selling book *The Shack*) there is a conversation between the comatose Tony and Jesus. In that conversation, Tony, who had lived a terrible life, is confronted by walls. He asks, "But don't I need walls?" Jesus explains that everyone needs boundaries, but not walls! Then He compares boundaries to the ocean and the shore. They are different and separate, but you can see the beauty in them both.[1]

All of us have erected walls in our souls that hinder others from seeing who we really are! Unfortunately, walls block your view of others. What one may view as protection often limits their vision. In 2 Corinthians 10:4–5, St. Paul speaks of strongholds or fortresses in one's mind, which he calls imaginations and thoughts. These walls, erected high enough, keep one from truly knowing God.

Later Paul would speak of the walls coming down between people and God, and between people and others.

But now in Christ Jesus you who once were far off have been brought near by the blood of Christ.

For He Himself is our peace, who has made both one, and has broken down the middle wall of separation, having abolished in His flesh the enmity, that is, the law of commandments contained in ordinances, so as to create in Himself one new man from the two, thus making peace, and that He might reconcile them both to God in one body through the cross, thereby putting to death the enmity. And He came and preached peace to you who were afar off and to those who were near. For through Him we both have access by one Spirit to the Father.

—Ephesians 2:13–18

Could it be that during the Crucifixion when the veil in the temple was torn in two from top to bottom, it represented the wall between man and God?

Perhaps it also represents the walls in our own hearts that keep us from knowing one another. The rending of the veil removes the barriers between knowing God, ourselves, and others.

Robert Frost wrote long ago, "Something there is that doesn't love a wall."[2] Ronald Reagan would look at Russian Premier Mikhail Gorbachev and say about the wall separating East and West Berlin, "Mr. Gorbachev, tear down this wall."[3]

At the cross Jesus is saying to us all, "Take down those walls." When we look at our world, and even the church that seems to reflect its values, we see walls! Look at Congress and the political system that is so divided. Our government is paralyzed by division.

Look at the home, with approximately half of all marriages ending in divorce. The landscape of the family is littered with the broken lives of children. Generational curses flow like a muddy river throughout all society.

Christianity offers very little escape from this climate. Denominationalism, legalism, jealousy, and partisan spirits divide church from church.

Racism is still among us, though hidden, its stench still wafts up into our daily lives.

What are these walls that rise between us? Can they be brought down?

Long ago the children of Israel marched around the walls of Jericho seven times and with a shout they crumbled to the earth!

As we close this book, I call on you to join me in that march to see these ancient walls fall!

NOTES

PROLOGUE: IN REMEMBRANCE OF DIETRICH BONHOEFFER

1. Dietrich Bonhoeffer, *The Cost of Discipleship* (New York: Touchstone, 1995), 89.
2. Eric Metaxas, *Bonhoeffer* (Nashville, TN: Thomas Nelson, 2010).
3. Dietrich Bonhoeffer, *Life Together* (New York, NY: HarperOne, 2009).

SECTION ONE: BEGINNING THE JOURNEY TO AGREEMENT

1. Thomas Moore, *Soul Mates* (New York: HarperPerennial, 1994), 256.

CHAPTER 2: THE EMPTINESS WE SHARE

1. Biography.com, "Hank Williams Biography," http://www.biography.com/people/hank-williams-9532414 (accessed January 23, 2014).
2. Ibid.

SECTION TWO: AGREEMENT WITH GOD

1. Moore, *Soul Mates*, 257.
2. Richard Greene, "Albert Einstein and the Scientific Proof of 'God,'" *Huffington Post*, January 1, 2011,

www.huffingtonpost.com/mobileweb/richardgreene/
alberteinstein-and-the-s_b_800936.html (accessed
January 22, 2014).

3. *Encyclopedia Britannica*, s.v. "olam ha-ze," http://
www.britannica.com/EBchecked/topic/426712/olam
Ha-ze (accessed January 23, 2014).

4. Judaism 101, "Kabbalah and Jewish Mysticism,"
http://www.jewfaq.org/m/kabbalah.htm (accessed
January 23, 2014).

5. Ariela Pelaia, "All About Judaism: 10 Of the Most
Commonly Asked Questions About Judaism," About
.com, http://judaism.about.com/od/judaismbasics/a/
All-About-Judaism-10-Common-Questions.htm
(accessed January 22, 2014).

CHAPTER 4: THE QUEST FOR AGREEMENT WITH GOD

1. For more information on Martin Luther see Christian Classics Ethereal Library, "Martin Luther:
German Reformer," http://m.ccel.org/browse/
authorInfo?id=luther (accessed January 23, 2014).

2. Ibid.

CHAPTER 5: BENEFITS TO LIVING IN AGREEMENT WITH GOD

1. ScienceDaily.com, "Indian Ocean Tsunami Warning
System Up and Running," July 10, 2007, http://www
.sciencedaily.com/releases/2006/07/060710085816
.htm (accessed January 23, 2014).

2. Micah Cobb, "John Wesley's Prayer Life," Thinking and Believing, July 27, 2013, http://micahcobb.com/blog/john-wesleys-prayer-life/ (accessed January 23, 2014).

3. Skip Bayless, "Radio Host Prefers Class Over Crass," *Chicago Tribune*, January 1, 2001, http://articles.chicagotribune.com/2001-01-10/sports/0101100167_1_cuban-jerry-reinsdorf-paying (accessed January 23, 2014).

4. Ibid.

CHAPTER 7: FIRST STEPS WITH GOD

1. *Thelma & Louise*, directed by Ridley Scott (1991; Santa Monica, CA: MGM Home Entertainment, 2004), DVD.

2. Brennan Manning, *Abba's Child* (Colorado Springs, CO: NavPress, 2002), 26–27.

CHAPTER 9: AGREEMENT STARTS IN YOUR HOME

1. Emerson Eggerichs, *Love and Respect* (Nashville, TN: Thomas Nelson, 2004), 5.

2. Wetshadows, "Check Out These Startling Statistics on TV Consumption in America," February 27, 2011, http://tinyurl.com/6j4vl77 (accessed March 18, 2014).

Chapter 10: Beyond You and Yours

1. BrainyQuote.com, "John Quincy Adams Quotes," http://www.brainyquote.com/quotes/quotes/j/ johnquincy386752.html (accessed January 23, 2014).

2. ThinkExist.com, "John J. Pershing Quotes," http:// thinkexist.com/quotation/a_competent_leader_can_ get_efficient_service_from/151512.html (accessed January 23, 2014).

3. William Shakespeare, "As It Fell Upon a Day," Sonnets to Sundry Notes of Music, VI, *The Oxford Shakespeare: Poems*, Bartleby.com, http://www .bartleby.com/70/536.html (accessed January 24, 2014).

4. Heard by the author from J. Willard Marriott at a Marriott hotel opening, New Orleans, LA, 1972.

5. BrainyQuote.com, "Paul Ryan Quote," http://www .brainyquote.com/quotes/quotes/p/paulryan440783 .html (accessed January 24, 2014).

6. Quoty.org, "Quote by Lieutenant Colonel Harold G. 'Hal' Moore," http://www.quoty.org/quote/5922 (accessed January 24, 2014).

7. Kevin Kruse, "Zig Ziglar: 10 Quotes That Can Change your Life," Forbes.com, http://www.forbes .com/sites/kevinkruse/2012/11/28/zig-ziglar-10 -quotes-that-can-change-your-life/ (accessed January 24, 2014).

8. BrainyQuote.com, "Aristotle Quote," http://www .brainyquote.com/quotes/quotes/a/aristotle105270 .html (accessed January 24, 2014).

9. Bartleby.com, "Robert South Quotes: 132," http://
www.bartleby.com/349/authors/185.html (accessed
January 24, 2014).

Chapter 12: The Hidden Power of Submission

1. Goodreads.com, "C. S. Lewis Quotes," http://www
.goodreads.com/quotes/437441-don-t-be-scared-by
-the-word-authority-believing-things-on (accessed
January 24, 2014).

2. Tolkiensociety.com, "R. R. Tolkien: a Biographical
Sketch," http://www.tolkiensociety.org/tolkien/
biography.html (accessed January 24, 2014).

3. MovieQuotesandMore.com, *The Hobbit: An Unexpected Journey* Quotes, http://www.moviequotes
andmore.com/an-unexpected-journey-quotes.html
(accessed January 24, 2014).

4. *The Hobbit: An Unexpected Journey*, directed by Peter
Jackson (N.p.: New Line Cinema, Metro-Goldwin-
Mayer, Wingnut Films, 2012).

Chapter 13: Dynamic Connections: The Jesus Model

1. BrainyQuote.com, "Ralph Waldo Emerson Quote,"
http://www.brainyquote.com/quotes/quotes/r/ralph
waldo105261.html (accessed January 24, 2014).

2. QuoteWorld.com, "Oliver Wendell Holmes Quote,"
http://www.quoteworld.org/quotes/12300 (accessed
January 24, 2014).

3. Ira Byock, *The Four Things That Matter Most* (New York, NY: Free Press, 2004).

Chapter 14: Genuine Agreement

1. Margalit Fox, "George Beverly Shea Dies at 104; Stirring Singer at Billy Graham Revivals," NYTimes.com, April 17, 2013, http://www.nytimes.com/2013/04/18/arts/music/george-beverly-shea-billy-grahams-singer-dies-at-104.html?_r=0 (accessed January 24, 2014).

2. Alice Gray, comp., *Stories for the Heart* (Sisters, OR: Multnomah, 2001), 27.

3. Bryan Smith, "A Test of Faith," in Jack Canfield, Mark Victor Hansen, Mark Donnelly, Chrissy Donnelly, Barbara De Angelis eds. *Chicken Soup for the Couple's Soul* (N.p: Open Road Media, 2012).

4. ThinkExist.com, "Henry David Thoreau Quotes," http://thinkexist.com/quotation/the_most_i_can_do_for_my_friend_is_simply_to_be/7806.html (accessed January 24, 2014).

Chapter 15: Agreement in the Family of God

1. ThinkExist.com, "Mark Twain Quotes," http://thinkexist.com/quotation/the_proper_office_of_a_friend_is_to_side_with_you/215218.html (accessed January 24, 2014).

2. Ruth Smalley, ed., *The Good Life Almanac* (Boone, NC: Appalachian Consortium Press, 1975). Out of print.

3. Robert Louis Stevenson, *Lay Morals and Other Papers* (London: Chatto & Windus, 1911).

EPILOGUE: BOUNDARIES, NOT WALLS

1. William Paul Young, *Cross Roads* (New York: Hachette Book Group, 2012).

2. Robert Frost, "Mending Wall," as quoted in Louis Untermeyer, ed., *Modern American Poetry* (New York: Harcourt, Brace & Howe, 1919; Bartleby.com, 1999), Bartleby.com, http://www.bartleby.com/104/64.html (accessed March 20, 2014).

3. Associated Press, "Reagan's 'Tear Down This Wall' Speech Turns 20," June 12, 2007, *USA Today*, http://usatoday30.usatoday.com/news/world/2007-06-12-reagan-speech_N.htm (accessed March 17, 2004).

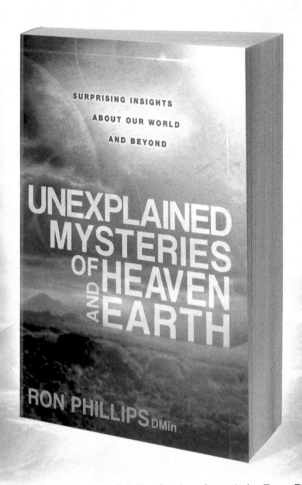

FREE NEWSLETTERS
TO HELP EMPOWER YOUR LIFE

Why subscribe today?

❏ **DELIVERED DIRECTLY TO YOU.** All you have to do is open your inbox and read.

❏ **EXCLUSIVE CONTENT.** We cover the news overlooked by the mainstream press.

❏ **STAY CURRENT.** Find the latest court rulings, revivals, and cultural trends.

❏ **UPDATE OTHERS.** Easy to forward to friends and family with the click of your mouse.

CHOOSE THE E-NEWSLETTER THAT INTERESTS YOU MOST:

- Christian news
- Daily devotionals
- Spiritual empowerment
- And much, much more

SIGN UP AT: **http://freenewsletters.charismamag.com**

8178